Nature's Wonders

*No one will protect what they don't
care about, and no one will care about
what they have never experienced.*

SIR DAVID ATTENBOROUGH

Nature's Wonders

Moments that Mark the Seasons

Jane V. Adams

 National Trust

For my mum, Joyce,

who showed me how to notice

Published by National Trust Books
An imprint of HarperCollins Publishers
1 London Bridge Street, London SE1 9GF
www.harpercollins.co.uk

HarperCollins Publishers
Macken House, 39/40 Mayor Street Upper, Dublin 1, D01 C9W8, Ireland

First published 2023

ISBN 978-1-91-165752-1
10 9 8 7 6 5 4 3 2 1

A catalogue record for this book is available from the British Library.

Printed and bound in Latvia

If you would like to comment on any aspect of this book, please contact us at
the above address or national.trust@harpercollins.co.uk

National Trust publications are available at National Trust shops or online at
nationaltrustbooks.co.uk

This book is produced from independently certified FSC™ paper
to ensure responsible forest management.

For more information visit: www.harpercollins.co.uk/green

Contents

Introduction   6

Spring   8

Summer   46

Autumn   88

Winter   130

Index   172

Picture Credits   176

Introduction

Storm clouds roll in across the stubble fields. Rain falls, and as it hits the sun-cracked soil, it releases a scent as old as the earth. Scientists called it petrichor: petra, meaning stone, and ichor, meaning ethereal fluid. This wild, fresh aroma would have been recognisable to our ancestors, and in an instant, and inexplicably, I find myself breathing deeper and feeling calmer.

Special moments like this can take us by surprise. Although nature doesn't exist solely for our benefit, it still has a knack of lifting us when we need it most. The wind, the rain, the scurrying clouds. Tawny owls who-hooing and ker-wicking. Bats catching mosquitoes in the warm, damp air, their wings flapping so fast and so close we can hear them. They're simple things. Simple moments. Yet experiencing them reminds us nature isn't something separate or out of reach. It's here, now, entwined throughout our lives.

Sometimes, though, we forget. Glued to screens and digital devices, we can become engrossed in, and exhausted by, the modern world and the pressures that come with it. We forget to go in search of shooting stars in the winter skies, or listen for the garden robin's serenade whilst putting out the bins. When was the last time you got down on your hands and knees and smelt the first bluebells of spring?

This book is about taking time to discover, or rediscover, our hidden wild wonders. Some are still relatively easy to encounter, such as wary slow worms, ready to sacrifice their tails to escape predation, and the wolf spider, carrying its young upon its back. Others, like the increase in autumn gales and growing rarity of snow and frost, are caused by our warming climate. Most we take for granted, but once noticed and experienced, they can remain forever as treasured memories.

Common darter dragonfly

It might sound too good to be true. In today's world, everything seems to demand hours of our time or money, or require expert skills. Yet, these moments are still here, hidden in plain view in the smallest gardens and busiest parks, in thousands of green spaces across the country and in the skies above and seas below.

As Octavia Hill, co-founder of the National Trust, said: 'We all want quiet. We all want beauty … We all need space. Unless we have it, we cannot reach that sense of quiet in which whispers of better things come to us gently.'

I hope this book helps you find the peace, beauty and space you need, and that by looking closer, discovering more and breathing just a little bit deeper, your life is enriched by the wonders of nature.

Jane Adams

SPRING

A time to nest

There is a hint of warmth. Trees are bursting into bud and there is the hum of a queen bumblebee emerging from her winter sleep. We rejoice at the subtle hints of spring, and we're not alone. Across the country, birds have been choosing mates, staking claim to territories and readying themselves for the most important time of their year: the breeding season.

For some, like the blue tit, timing is everything. Unlike blackbirds or robins that breed several times a year, blue tits typically have just one chance. It is vital their eggs hatch at the same time as the juicy caterpillars on which their young rely for food. Blue tits seem to have two main ways of determining when this will be: night-time temperatures and budburst.

Blue tits are less likely to nest or lay eggs if night temperatures are low in spring. A shrewd tactic, as the female will need to keep her eggs at around 38°C during incubation. Cold night-time temperatures would make successful incubation a lot harder, perhaps even impossible.

Research indicates that blue tits use the timing of leaf budburst of birch trees – a common tree that comes into leaf earlier than most – as an indicator to begin nesting. If this is true, it would be some of the first evidence of birds using a specific tree as a cue for breeding. With many bird species breeding up to 31 days earlier than they did in the 1960s, due to climate change, this strategy might be helping blue tits stay in sync with their important food sources.

Egg-laying is an arduous and energy-draining task for any bird. But with each of her 12 or so eggs, weighing 1g apiece, a 10g (⅓oz) blue tit will lay more than her own body weight in eggs. After laying an egg each day for up to two weeks, she needs to incubate them as quickly as possible to protect them from predators.

*A blue tit will lay
more than her own body
weight in eggs.*

The female blue tit has two things in her favour: courtship feeding and a brood patch. By plucking feathers from her breast and belly to provide a highly vascular patch of skin – called a brood patch – she's able to regulate the eggs' incubation temperature. And if she doesn't need to stop to feed herself, and is instead fed by her mate (a service he also performs during courtship and while the eggs are being laid), the eggs are likely to hatch quicker, and more chicks are likely to fledge.

We can help too. Findings suggest that when blue tits are fed high-quality supplementary food – such as mealworms and wax moth larvae – parents have more time to forage for natural foods and bring back larger food items for their chicks. This extra 'easy' food may also allow the parents more time to defend their territory, watch out for predators and look after themselves. With each chick needing on average 100 caterpillars a day for up to three weeks, this might give these avian workaholics a well-earned rest.

If you don't currently have blue tits nesting in your garden, now is a great time to consider putting up some bird boxes. There are many online guides to making your own, but you could also invest in a good quality, ready-made bird box from a local garden centre.

Budburst

As spring wanders from south to north at a leisurely pace of one to two kilometres an hour, leaf buds usually burst on our trees and shrubs between March and May. The sticky buds of horse chestnut are among the first to show, whereas others, such as ash, can be very slow to get going. We presume buds are a sign of trees waking up. In reality, they were never asleep. Even in winter, they are monitoring the temperature, how much water they have and the length of the days, waiting for the perfect time to start growing again. Most trees need a sustained period of cold before this can take place. Called vernalisation, this prevents the tree from being fooled into leafing during periods of warmer winter weather, when it's really too early. When the time is right, leaves emerge from buds produced the previous summer and autumn, and hormones such as auxin and cytokinin leap into action to encourage cell division and growth.

Phenology, the science of recording when events such as budburst happen, has long been a source of fascination. In Japan, the date when cherry tree blossom peaks has been documented for over 1,000 years, and records of crop yields in China are thought to date back to 974 BC. An early record-keeper of phenological events in the UK was naturalist Robert Marsham, who started noting down the 'Indications of Spring' in 1736. It was a tradition his family continued for nearly 200 years.

More recently, since the year 2000, the Centre for Ecology and Hydrology and the Woodland Trust have been running Nature's Calendar, a citizen-led science project which collects records from the first hawthorn budburst to when oaks lose their leaves. The project has attracted thousands of participants, and the millions of records collected are now helping scientists determine the impact of climate change and weather on wildlife. They have already noted that a 1°C increase in

> *We presume buds are a sign of trees waking up. In reality, they were never asleep.*

temperatures in March or April is linked to buds bursting between four and six days earlier, and that temperatures between 2000 and 2016 were, on average, 1.2°C warmer than between 1961 and 1990. If you factor in light pollution, late frosts and the 10 warmest years on record since 2005, then there is little doubt that plants will struggle to stay in sync with the insects on which they rely and vice versa. Caterpillars emerging when leaves are old and tough won't be as healthy, leading to less food for blue tit chicks. Trees that flower early won't be pollinated, while insects hatching at the 'normal' time won't find the pollen they need to feed their young.

To identify different trees from their leaf buds, there are a few things you can look out for. Trees with a terminal bud on the end of each stem include horse chestnut, maple, ash, aspen and walnut. Buds along the stem (lateral buds) that are opposite one another can be found on ash, dogwood, spindle and sycamore, whereas alternate buds occur on rowan, hawthorn, hazel, goat willow, hornbeam, alder, beech, walnut and London plane. Individual buds that seem to spiral around the stem are probably oak, blackthorn or aspen, and those with a zig-zag formation, elms and limes. Clusters of lateral or terminal buds are found on wild cherry, blackthorn and oaks. And look out for the distinctive hairy buds on rowan, field maple and hazel.

The saying 'ash before oak, we're in for a soak; oak before ash, we're in for a splash', though occasionally correct, has never held much water. Oak buds have nearly always burst before ash, and continue to do so, but instead of a splash, we may now experience flash floods or prolonged dry summers.

Five buds to find

- **Beech** - Buds are thin, long and pointed with copper-brown colouring.

- **Oak** - Buds are oval with a blunt end in a cluster; usually orange-brown.

- **Hazel** - Short buds with hairy, green-red scales. Stems are also hairy.

- **Elder** - Buds look like miniature pineapples; their scales are spiky and dark red, in opposite pairs.

- **Ash** - Found in opposite pairs. Rounded on the stems, the buds are dark red or black in colour. The tips of the shoots have a distinctive upward bend.

Beech

Oak

Ash

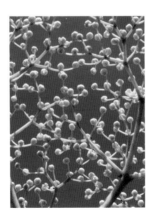

Elder

Hazel

Brimstone butterflies

B rimstone is an old term for sulphur, and the male brimstone butterfly with its bright, acid yellow wings certainly lives up to its elemental name. No wonder brimstone or the Old English, *brynstān*, also means 'burning stone'.

If you've ever tried to watch a brimstone in the spring, you'll know how apt its name is. Like a flickering flame, it jerks and flutters, disappears, reappears and flits around. It goes to land, then changes its mind and flies high into the sky, like a wind-borne ember. Frenetic doesn't do this butterfly justice. Following it, for just a few seconds, leaves you feeling exhausted.

It has been suggested that the buttery yellow brimstone could even be the origin of the word 'butterfly'. They can be seen for much of the year (they often have a second brood in the summer); they can emerge from their slumber on warm, sunny winter days, and they are conspicuous in spring. Therefore, it is perhaps reasonable to suggest a brimstone could have been the original butter-coloured fly.

Both males and females are experts at camouflage, which, for such a brightly coloured butterfly, is a surprising talent. The females are a much less conspicuous whitish green compared to the showy yellow males, but both are good at hiding. When they perch, they hold their vein-marked, leaf-shaped wings folded above their back and miraculously seem to disappear. This is certainly fortunate, because in winter they tuck themselves away within the foliage of holly, bramble and ivy, and many will manage to stay safe from predation until they are ready to emerge and mate during the first warm days of spring.

However, they may be struggling to survive. In 2021, Butterfly Conservation's Big Butterfly Count reported that brimstone numbers had

> *When they perch, they hold their vein-marked, leaf-shaped wings folded above their back and miraculously seem to disappear.*

fallen by a third on previous years. Though this was only one year, it does seem to be part of a worrying trend for butterflies. In 2021, Butterfly Conservation's annual survey received more butterfly counts than ever before, yet the numbers recorded during each count were the lowest they'd ever been. We know that some butterflies have been declining for years but now, because of habitat loss and extreme temperature changes, experts are worried some common species could become rarities.

Though brimstones are pushing north, you're most likely to see them south of a line between Cheshire and south-east Yorkshire. As they're one of the longest tongued butterflies, you'll often find them feeding from flowers with deep nectaries, such as bluebells and primroses, as well as on other early spring flowers such as dandelions and bugles. Females lay eggs on buckthorn, their caterpillar's food plant. Look out for females laying individual eggs on the underside of the youngest leaves of purging or alder buckthorn. The bright yellow males are on the wing from March. However, warm temperatures before then can sometimes draw them out of hiding much earlier. In 2022, some were recorded on New Year's Day, a reminder that you might spot this special butter-coloured fly at any time of the year.

Dandelions

The *Cambridge Dictionary* defines a weed as 'any wild plant that grows in an unwanted place'. Is the dandelion a weed? Many people nowadays regard it as such, but that hasn't always been the case.

Its common name is derived from the French *dent-de-lion*, meaning 'lion's tooth', a reference to the plant's jagged-toothed leaves. Yet its blooms are probably its most recognisable feature, with poet John Clare once describing them as 'shining like guineas' – an apt description for a flower that looks as if it could have been dipped in gold.

There are over 200 species of dandelion in the UK and Ireland. It's a remarkably diverse plant and, before lawnmowers and the popularity of lawns, was deeply valued. Indeed, the plant was given extra space in our gardens and prized for its culinary uses. Young leaves were used in salads and blanched like spinach; flowers were fermented and made into wine or a light mead; its roots could be dried and roasted to make a (vaguely coffee-like) coffee substitute. It was even used in ancient remedies to treat upset stomachs and skin conditions. But as its medicinal properties fell out of favour and the craze for manicured lawns took hold, we tried to eliminate the dandelion from our gardens and its status as a weed grew and grew.

However, opinions are gradually changing. We now recognise that pollinators such as bumblebees, hoverflies and solitary bees thrive on the early nectar and pollen of the dandelion. A host of invertebrates, such as muslin and ruby tiger moth caterpillars, make use of the plant's leaves as a food source. Look closely and you'll even see tiny pollen beetles buried deep within the flower's florets. Instead of grabbing a trowel and digging them out, or worse, reaching for a bottle of weedkiller, gardeners are now leaving dandelions to benefit nature.

Bumblebees, hoverflies and solitary bees thrive on the early nectar and pollen of the dandelion.

They aren't the only ones looking at dandelions with fresh eyes. Researchers interested in biomimicry (design and technology inspired by nature) have noticed how dandelion seeds can float long distances on the lightest of breezes, and have designed wind-blown sensors. Tiny and wireless, their seed-inspired sensors can relay valuable information on temperature, pressure, humidity and light without the need for a battery. In the future, it is hoped this technology can be used to monitor isolated or fragile regions of the world that are difficult to reach on foot, and would be easily damaged by humans.

Dandelions could also change the way we produce one of our most used commodities – rubber. Pick any dandelion flower and you'll notice a sticky residue oozing from its stalk. This latex contains the same compounds as *Hevea brasiliensis*, the rubber tree (the source of natural rubber). However, unlike rubber tree latex, potentially polluting solvents are not required for its extraction, and it can be grown in relatively poor soils in temperate climates, thus reducing transportation costs.

The lion-toothed leaves of the dandelion are also high in vitamins, calcium, manganese and potassium, so will add a mineral punch to any meal. Plus, a few sunshine petals will brighten any summer salad and are a natural diuretic used to treat water retention. As the flowers fade, don't forget to make a wish as you blow on the spherical seedheads, watching as they float away on the breeze. It's said that dandelion seeds carry thoughts and dreams to loved ones, which is as good a reason as any to grow and respect them. As Canadian author Heather Babcock says, 'dandelions are just friendly little weeds who only want to be loved like flowers.'

Blackcaps

As a nation, we spend an estimated £250 million pounds a year on 150,000 tonnes of bird food. For many of us with access to outside space, refilling the bird feeder has become part of our everyday lives. Birds are regular visitors who seem like old friends. We relish the challenge of identifying, recording, painting and photographing them. In many ways, it's not surprising we invest in them: birdwatching is undoubtedly soothing. They represent a little bit of the wild, flying in and out of our lives, connecting us to the outside world.

However, regularly feeding our garden birds is a relatively new passion. In the 1970s, if you had a bird feeder – and they were rare – you might only have seen a handful of different birds. Nowadays, over 30 different species have been recorded regularly feeding at garden bird feeders. For many of these pampered avians, their populations are growing, sometimes at the expense of some of their relatives: thriving populations of blue tits and great tits are threatening the survival of the more vulnerable marsh tit.

One bird that has particularly benefited from garden feeders is the blackcap. This chunky little fellow is about the size of a great tit, but with longer legs and a fine, pointed beak. Most of its feathers are grey, except for a distinctive black (in males) or chestnut brown (in females and youngsters) skull cap, making it quite an easy bird to identify. Though you'll often hear one before you see it. In 1770, naturalist Gilbert White described its warbling song as being 'a songster of the first rate. Its notes are deep and sweet. Called in Norfolk the mock nightingale.' If, on the other hand, you disturb one, or it feels threatened, its harsh 'chac-chac' warnings are more like two stones clacking together.

The blackcap has been a summer migrant to the UK for hundreds of years. Traditionally, it has bred in woodlands, hedges and shrubs, where it feeds on insects. Then, before it migrates back to the Mediterranean and North Africa in the autumn, it changes its diet, boosting energy reserves by eating sugary wild fruits.

There have always been a few winter hangers-on, and it was presumed some just didn't bother flying south. But over the last 50 years, the numbers spotted during winter have slowly increased. However, these winter birds aren't the same as our summer visitors. We now know that, instead of heading south, birds that breed in southern Germany and Austria are heading north-west to the UK for the winter, which is very unusual behaviour. Initially, this change in migration pattern was probably because of our warming climate, but it's now been shown that it is also our passion for feeding them that has led to this winter increase. Whereas previously they would have fed on hedgerow fruits during the colder months, they now gravitate towards urban and suburban gardens, where there is a regular supply of fat and sunflower seeds.

Astonishingly, this has led to physical changes in the birds: because these winter blackcaps know where their next meal is coming from, they can now afford to carry smaller fat stores. This makes them more agile and possibly harder for predators to catch. They also don't have as far to fly to return to their summer breeding grounds in Europe and, on average, they are arriving up to 10 days earlier than their competitors. This has led not only to them getting the pick of the breeding sites and the healthiest mates, but also to the likelihood of more fledglings.

Next time you see these charismatic and adaptable birds on your bird feeder in winter, you will know that you have helped them become a more common sight in our gardens.

Slow worms

There are six species of cold-blooded reptile native to the UK. They include three snakes – adder, grass and smooth – and three lizards: the common and sand lizard, and the slow worm. Some, like the smooth snake and sand lizard, are rare and live in specialist heathland habitats, but of the rest, our reptile equivalent of the hedgehog is the slow worm. Some may argue they're not as appealing as the prickly mammal, but this cold-blooded creature has adapted to our human-made habitats, and, like the hedgehog, is rather helpful.

Also known as 'deaf adder', 'blind worm' and 'long-cripple', slow worms are not actually deaf, blind, long, slow or even worms. When Shakespeare's witches in *Macbeth* threw 'blind-worm's sting' into their cauldron, they believed the slow worm's small eyes and snake-like appearance meant it was blind and could somehow sting. It isn't and it can't. If handled gently, they're totally harmless.

As well as railway embankments, road verges, fields, woodland edges and brownfield sites, they live in the wilder areas of allotments and back gardens. To see a slow worm is always a thrill and feels strangely exotic, even though they can be found all over England, Scotland and Wales.

Their name is thought to come from the Old English *slāwyrm*; *slā* from the Swedish for 'earthworm' and *wyrm* meaning 'legless dragon'. Their interlocking scales can be the colour of burnished gold or smoky grey, with some males even having blue spots. When it hibernates in the winter, its smooth skin helps it burrow underground or deep into compost heaps, only emerging when the weather warms up in spring.

Though it looks snake-like, there are some fundamental differences – the most obvious is that it has eyelids and can blink, which is something snakes can't do. Its tongue is notched, rather than forked, and it is also

A slow worm's last line of defence against a
would-be attacker is to detach its tail.

---

smaller than most common snakes, with a maximum length of around 50cm (20in) when fully grown. Whereas an adult grass snake can reach 90–150cm (35–60in). As well as spiders and earthworms, the slow worm lives on a varied diet including snails and slugs – which makes it a gardener's friend.

The slow worm in your garden may have lived there for longer than you thought. With an average lifespan in the wild thought to be between 20 and 30 years, they're one of the longest-lived lizards. In fact, a captive slow worm at Copenhagen Zoo lived until it was 54 years old.

This longevity is probably down to a few clever adaptations. The slow worm's first defence against being caught is either to stay stock still – and hope it isn't seen – or quickly slither away. If that doesn't work, it defecates. Though smelly and messy, this is not always enough to put off a would-be attacker, which is when it performs its *pièce de résistance*, and detaches its tail.

As the eighteenth-century naturalist Gilbert White observed, 'While you are looking at the tail wriggling and jumping about, the body quietly makes its escape.' In this process, known as caudal autotomy, the tail does grow back eventually, but is shorter than before. Studies show that 50–70 per cent of slow worms in the UK have at one time lost a tail.

The best way to see this gentle reptile is to make your garden as slow worm-friendly as possible. They give birth in places like compost heaps in August and September to up to 12 black or dark-brown live young (the eggs hatch inside the female before birth). The adults don't tend to lie out in the open; instead, you're more likely to see them curled up under something warm. If you place a few pieces of corrugated iron or 1sq. m (11sq. ft) sheets of bitumen-backed roofing material in full sun next to thick undergrowth, you'll be providing them with a safe place to maintain their body temperature. It also gives you the opportunity to look at them, but don't check underneath too often. They're easily disturbed, so be extra careful not to squash or trap them when replacing the covering, ideally no more than once a week.

Though slow worms are thought to be common and are protected by British law against deliberately being injured or killed, there is still relatively little known about them. Using fewer, or preferably no, pesticides will ensure they aren't poisoned, and their prey can flourish. If we want to continue seeing these charismatic creatures in the future, we'll need to protect their garden habitats as much as possible.

Bee-flies

Bee-flies love the heat. To spot your first one of the year, look no further than your feet. Warm spring days are the perfect time to see one. When perched motionless on last year's autumn leaves, with their long spindly legs holding their furry bodies aloft, they have a certain cuteness about them, but in a slightly alien way. This is due to the narwhal-like tusk protruding from their faces. This is actually a long, rigid tongue, called a proboscis, that they use when feeding. When they fly, a pair of near-invisible cellophane wings beat so fast it makes them look as if they're levitating.

While newly emerged bumblebee queens bounce between plants, bee-flies negotiate them with the poise of a catwalk model. They hover, then move, then hover some more without a hair or leg out of place. Though their appearance may suggest they could sting, they can't. They are a harmless fly. The bee-fly's mimicry of a bee is thought to protect them from predators who seem just as confounded as we are by their similarity.

To distinguish between males and females, look at their eyes. If they meet at the top, you'll know it's a male. If there's a gap, it's a female. But if you can't get that close (which can be tricky with this nippy insect), watch its behaviour if a rival bee-fly approaches. A dominant male will chase it away, claiming your green patch, and any flowers and female bee-flies within it, as his own. Whereas females will probably carry on feeding with their long proboscises plunged into flowers, hovering in front of them like miniature hummingbirds.

As spring progresses, you might witness other interesting behaviours, but beware. This is when the bee-fly's habits start to get a little macabre. If you see a female flying low over the lawn, she's probably looking for

Though their appearance may suggest
they could sting, they can't.
They are a harmless fly.

mining bee nests – small round volcanos of earth in the soil. On finding one, she will flick her own eggs onto the ground nearby and once hatched, her grubs will wiggle their way deep into the bee's nest. Here they'll devour the bee larvae and bee's pollen supplies, before pupating and emerging as adults the next spring.

Though this seems bad news for the bees, bee-flies are just one of many parasites the bees have co-existed with over millions of years. The bee-fly's habits may be unsavoury but humans are still bees' worst enemy. From the climate crisis to killing wildflowers with an overuse of pesticides, we pose a far greater threat to our beleaguered wild bee populations than the humble bee-fly.

There are 10 species of bee-fly in the UK, but by far the most widespread and the one you're most likely to see is the dark-edged bee-fly. As its name suggests, it has a dark, wavy edge to its wings, which makes it relatively easy to identify, especially when it comes to rest and stretches them out at right angles for all to see.

If you're keen to spot one, keep an eye on the weather. Bee-flies love warm, dry temperatures, and though the dark-edged bee-fly has been seen in February, you're most likely to see one in March or April. If you have flowers in your garden, or in your local green space, these delicate pollinators are sure to find them. Pay careful attention to plants that bloom near to the ground, especially primroses, bugles, pulmonaria and wood anemones, and you won't be disappointed.

The first solitary bees

A small mound of soil appears in the middle of the lawn, a miniature version of the volcano that emerged in a Mexican cornfield in 1943. This mini-Parícutin is barely the size of a buttercup flower. At 1cm (almost ½in) high, and with a pencil-sized hole in the centre, it could be mistaken for a worm cast. But there's something about it that hints it could be more interesting – and then a bee crawls out.

If you could describe any insect as glamorous, then this stunner would fit the bill. Wrapped in a sumptuous foxy-red coat, a face and legs as dark as coal, and with a decidedly curvy figure, she (because this insect oozes femininity) has all the glamour of a film star. As she flies low over the grass and disappears into the hole, you wonder how you've never noticed her before.

Female tawny mining bee

This is a solitary bee, a female tawny mining bee. They are called solitary because, unlike bumblebees and honeybees, these bees don't tend to be social and mainly nest alone. She's one of 250 or so solitary bee species that call the UK home. Adults only live a few weeks. Some are minuscule and look more like hairless wasps. Others are so rare you're unlikely to ever come across them.

Several that you might see in your garden have intriguing common names. There's the hairy-footed flower bee, the male of which does indeed have very hairy legs. The wool carder bee, that combs hairs from plants to use as nesting material, and the ashy mining bee, that looks quite un-bee-like dressed in its black-and-white hairy suit.

Female solitary bees are usually easier to identify and are larger than the males, and because many of them collect pollen on their legs or abdomen, easier to spot. Most are also docile and non-threatening. You can sit among them as they collect nectar and pollen from garden flowers, and they won't take the least bit of notice of you.

You'll often find them nesting in flowerbeds, plant pots, lawns, wood piles and walls. Most of the time, you wouldn't even know they are there. But in places where their nesting habitats are more limited, some species, such as red mason bees and leaf-cutter bees, will use artificial nests such as 'bee hotels' filled with hollow bamboo or special bee-sized straws. You can make or buy a bee hotel to put up in your garden, and when spring arrives, you can watch the bees move in. Beware though, it's addictive viewing.

The telltale soil eruptions made by the tawny mining bee as she digs her nest in your lawn or flowerbeds should be easy to spot. Or you might see her nemesis, the dark-edged bee-fly who will try to flick her own eggs near to the mining bee's nest. Once hatched, they crawl into the bee's nest, eat her young and consume any food reserves.

In April, May and June it's also worth looking for solitary bees as they collect nectar and pollen from flowers. Pay particular attention to apple blossom, bluebells, forget-me-nots, pulmonaria and dandelions.

The differences between solitary bees and hoverflies

- Hoverflies tend to have short, stumpy antennae, while a bee's antennae are much longer.
- Bees have two pairs of wings. Hoverflies have only one pair, but this can be hard to spot as their wings move so quickly.
- Many of the common female solitary bees are hairy. Hoverflies, although excellent bee-mimics, are generally much less hairy and cute-looking.
- Bees have a more pronounced waspish waist. The waist of hoverflies is far less defined, some hardly going in at all at the waist.

Male wool carder bee

Wood anemones

There's a delicacy to wood anemones not found in other, sturdier-looking spring flowers, such as wild daffodils or primroses. Perhaps that's how they came by one of their common names, the windflower. The word 'anemone' comes from the Greek, meaning 'daughter of the wind', as the flowers were believed to only open when the wind blew, although this is not actually the case. A Greek legend tells of Anemos, the wind god, sending his namesakes the anemones before him in spring to herald his arrival. A woodland floor covered in white wood anemones is a completely different experience to seeing more colourful wildflowers, such as bluebells or wild daffodils; it's altogether more ethereal and delicate.

This is a sun-loving plant, and blooms between March and May, while the tree canopy is leafless. It spreads by way of rhizomes, creeping rootstalks which grow at an agonisingly slow 1.8m (6ft) per 100 years. So, where wood anemones are found covering a woodland floor, it can indicate an ancient wood, a habitat that comprises just 2.5 per cent of the land in the UK. In some areas it is not unusual to come across small patches of 'woodland ghosts' – relics of long-forgotten ancient woods now reduced to a single tree. In Yorkshire, wood anemones can also be found growing in the shaded crevices on exposed limestone pavements. For a plant with a species name derived from the Latin *nemorosus*, meaning 'covered with trees', it's an unusual habitat in which to find what many regard as a woodland plant.

Wood anemones belong to the buttercup family and the blooms are usually white. But don't be caught out – in some counties, they can be tinged with pink or purple, especially on the back of their six or seven petal-like sepals (the covering that protects the bud). Inside each flower,

bright yellow anthers float above a green centre.

Although they are poisonous to humans, the plant was once used in traditional remedies to treat gout, rheumatism and headaches. It is also shrouded in folklore. Romans would pick the first anemone flowers of the year to protect themselves from fever. In the Middle Ages, peasants wore them on their collars to ward off pestilence and disease and, if you needed a fairy at night, you'd be sure to find one tucked up inside an anemone flower.

Where wood anemones are found covering a woodland floor, it can indicate an ancient wood, a habitat that comprises just 2.5 per cent of the land in the UK.

Over the years, wood anemones have accumulated some wonderfully descriptive common names: moggie nightgown (in parts of Derbyshire, 'moggie' means 'mouse' rather than 'cat'), grandmother's nightcap, moonflower and thimbleweed are just a few.

The anemone flower produces pollen, but it wasn't thought to make nectar until scientists spotted dark-edged bee-flies feeding on the flowers in 2013 and decided to investigate. There, deep within the flower, they discovered tiny nectaries, although unless you were a long-tongued insect, like the bee-fly, you would struggle to find them. It just goes to show how little we actually know about our native flowers.

If you'd like to experience a display of wood anemones, they are not just found in ancient woodland, but can also be seen in parks, graveyards and gardens, as well as hedges, grassland and moorland. However, if you do spot a small cluster of them under a lone tree, remember that you might just be in the presence of a woodland ghost.

Dawn chorus

How are you with mornings, I mean really early mornings? Do you jump out of bed and fling open the windows, or do you dive back under the covers for another couple of hours? Even if you're a night owl, read on. The dawn chorus is one of the most uplifting natural moments you can experience, and even if it might not be your thing, listening at least once a year is well worth the effort.

It does need to be the right time of day and the right time of the year. You can venture out at dawn in the darkness of November, or in the squinting brightness of August, but though both are still pleasant, they won't be as eventful as April or May. These are the months when the dawn chorus really goes into overdrive. Though it's called the dawn

Wren

chorus, as far as the birds are concerned, harmony is not their primary concern. It's about power and sex, holding onto territory and attracting a mate. It's a giant audition to decide whose song is more desirable and who has the most extensive repertoire. This is about singing for a future for your eventual offspring. Singing for life itself.

From the highest vantage points, thrushes are often the first to start the chorus. The excited, repeated phrases of the song thrush and the confident but laid-back, fluted rise and fall of a blackbird often shatter the silence while it's still dark. As light creeps over the horizon, other birds join in. 'My toe bleeds, Betty', coos the wood pigeon as a jackdaw clack-clacks from a nearby chimney. And as the conductor-less symphony builds to a crescendo, house sparrows chirp, there's the stab of 'tea-cher, tea-cher' from a great tit and the firing of notes from a tiny wren – who has a song so loud it feels like it could pierce your skin. Throughout this cacophony, the robin's warbling, melancholic whistles and pauses sew the fabric of jumbled notes together.

International Dawn Chorus Day is celebrated on the first Sunday in May. To join in with the celebrations, you'll often find events organised by your local conservation group taking place nearby. But if you'd rather listen on your own, or with a few friends, try to get into position about an hour before dawn. With low light levels, it's still too dark for most birds to be foraging for food, so they sing instead.

It's about power and sex, holding onto territory and attracting a mate.

While listening, it can feel as if you're being bombarded. You might have difficulty keeping up and taking it all in. If each tune was the same distance away or at the same height, or if they sang one at a time, you might stand a chance. Instead, there are a hundred different tones, pitches and rhythms. The only sensible thing to do is to slow your breathing down and try to absorb it. All too soon the birdsong will fade away and stop as quickly as it started, leaving just another day ahead.

Every dawn chorus has its own character. Some will have multiple singers, others just a handful. But don't feel as if you need to identify every bird – this isn't a competition. You'll find that as you listen, you'll pick out different songs and characters, you may even recognise a few. Ultimately, though, just experiencing the moment is what really matters.

Robin

Wild blossom

The no-man's land between winter and spring can be a frustrating time for humans. But for nature, it signifies new life.

During the spring of 2020, many of us discovered or rediscovered a love for the natural world triggered by the sadness, restrictions and stress of the pandemic lockdowns. When we could escape the four walls of home on our daily walks we discovered new green spaces, and the rhythm of the changing seasons filled us with hope. That spring, blackthorn and hawthorn blossomed frosty white and cream in hedgerows and parks across the country, and it was as if we were seeing their blooms for the first time.

There was a time when we weren't so pleased to see blackthorn. In folklore, it was often associated with misfortune. Witches were thought to use its vicious thorns to prick their victims and to make wands from its wood. But our connection to this tree has existed for millennia; stones from sloes, the blackthorn's sour, blue-black fruit, were found in the stomach of a mummified Neolithic 'iceman' in the Alps. That's around 6,000 years ago.

Nowadays, we're more likely to use sloes to flavour a seasonal gin tipple, but the blackthorn's association with wildlife is arguably more symbiotic. Not only is the blossom a welcome source of early pollen and nectar for bumble and solitary bees, but as it drops, moth and butterfly caterpillars will also eat its sprouting leaves. And they, in turn, will become food for the young of birds nesting in its protective thorns. You could argue that blackthorn has its own mini ecosystem.

The spines of our other blossoming thorn bush, the hawthorn, are less severe than the blackthorn. Its pink-tinged froth of blooms arrive slightly later, in May, after its leaves. This has given rise to one of its common names, the May tree. In fact, the old saying, 'Cast ne'er a clout ere May is out,' warns us not to discard our winter clothing until the May tree blooms. Sound advice with the vagaries of British weather.

This is another tree that's steeped in symbolism. People would traditionally bring its blossom into their homes at Beltane – the Gaelic May Day festival – as it represented fertility and hope. Conversely, in medieval times, its flowers were the harbingers of illness and death if brought inside at any time other than Beltane. The hawthorn's connection to death has long intrigued botanists. When a compound found in rotting flesh – triethylamine – was discovered in its flowers, it is thought the smell must have reminded those who lived through the great plagues of the smell of death.

It's wise simply to appreciate all blossoms in the wild, rather than pick them. Whether it's blackthorn, hawthorn, crab apple or wild pear, you can't go wrong with bathing in the beauty of a blossom tree. In Japan, it's

Blackthorn

Hawthorn

called *Hanami*, which means 'flower viewing', and the charm of this annual natural event is widely celebrated.

We can do the same. Try to find a blossoming tree away from the hustle and bustle of everyday life and slow your mind and body down for a minute or two. Sit on the ground, if you can, and play with your senses. Do you hear the breeze whispering through the branches? Can you hear bees buzzing in the flowers or birds singing? When you look at the blossom, is the overall effect pure white or tinged with pink? Do individual flowers look the same and can you smell their scent?

You could write a poem, describe what you feel in a paragraph of creative writing, or sketch or paint what you see. No one else needs to see it and you might surprise yourself. If you'd like to share your experience with others, join the National Trust's #Blossomwatch on social media by sending in your recorded sounds, photographs or videos. That way, even more people can enjoy the experience.

Bluebells

There is a silent eloquence
In every wild bluebell

FROM 'THE BLUEBELL' (1838) BY ANNE BRONTË

It's a well-worn cliché, but the sight of a woodland floor covered in wild bluebells can stop you in your tracks. Physically, you might feel yourself relax, your shoulders slowly becoming less knotted and tense. Even though it may be raining, you might even smile. There's no getting away from it – English bluebells, especially when seen en masse, have a knack for making us happy.

The flowers, nodding their heads to the sides of drooping stems, look as if they're taking a bow. In dryer weather, their tubular blooms, with their flicked-up-at-the-end petals and subtle scent, will lure in brimstone butterflies and hairy-footed flower bees to feed. They are a valuable source of food for these early pollinators.

On a wet day, the bluebell's violet flowers swirl like water above blue-green leaves and take on a magical quality. A number of this plant's traditional names, from 'witches' thimbles' to 'fairy flowers', hint at a long association with magic.

Folklore warns us not to pick wild bluebells, as fairies will lead us astray, and you'll be compelled to tell the truth if you wear a bluebell garland. It seems we underestimate the mythological power of this plant at our peril, and that the fairies understood this plant's fragility. Although they are common, bluebells are so delicate that their thin leaves can become weak if trampled. It takes a staggering five to seven years for bluebell seeds to develop into bulbs and subsequently flower.

With almost 50 per cent of the world's wild bluebells growing in the

UK, it's reassuring to know it's illegal to remove plants from the wild. Nevertheless, they also require ancient woods and undisturbed land to grow and spread. Whether on an open clifftop, under a hedge or in a woodland, bluebells demand continuity, something our changing, human-made landscape sometimes struggles to provide. Suddenly, the conservation and protection of their habitat becomes even more important.

Our wild bluebells are also under attack from other quarters. Spanish bluebells and garden cultivars that once escaped over the garden wall may now pose a threat to our native population. Surveys by the wild plant and fungi charity Plantlife found Spanish bluebells growing in a sixth of the UK's broadleaved woodlands. Unless we can stop the crossbreeding and competitiveness of these invaders, our delicate, native flower may decline further.

Perhaps its long-term survival will rely on its usefulness. The Elizabethans once crushed bluebell bulbs to use as a stiffener for their ruffs; at one time the plant's sap was used as a glue for bookbinding as it repelled insects; and there was even

It takes a staggering five to seven years for bluebell seeds to develop into bulbs and subsequently flower.

tentative research in the 1990s to see whether the plant's biologically active compounds could be used in the treatment of HIV and cancer. But maybe its ultimate usefulness – though this word feels inappropriate for something so wild – lies in its ability to evoke positive emotions within us, so that a moment spent in a bluebell wood is guaranteed to make you smile.

It's best to pick an overcast day to appreciate a bluebell wood, as bright sunshine subdues their intense colour. Even a slight drizzle is fine. Find a wood with public access and clear footpaths, so you won't trample their delicate flowers or leaves. Close up, you will be able to see how each bluebell is unique. It is estimated one in ten thousand bluebells is white because of a genetic mutation. Feel their waxy, tubular blooms. Bend down and breathe their scent. Then take time to appreciate the scene. Listen for any natural sounds, such as birdsong or bees, and notice how the dark brown tree trunks contrast with the sea of iridescent purple flowers.

SUMMER

Foxgloves

Don't be fooled by this plant's beguiling beauty. As the old saying goes, it can 'raise the dead or kill the living'. Every part of a foxglove is heart-stoppingly poisonous. From its fibrous roots and velvet leaves, to the tips of its trumpeting blooms, it hides dark secrets.

Though its flowers may tempt bees to stop for a while, local names such as 'witches' thimbles' and 'dead man's bells' hint at a deep human knowledge of its deadly ways. In Northern England, it was thought the devil could enter your house if you brought foxgloves inside, and in Scotland mothers scattered its leaves around their baby's cradle for protection against bewitchment.

If, on the other hand, you want to attract fairies, you can plant foxgloves in your garden where, it's said, these little magical beings will leave their handprints on the flowers and make the stems bow as they walk pass.

Why they are called foxgloves is less clear. Although you'll often find the plants growing in profusion near to foxholes, the name is more likely to have originated from folklore. Legend says foxes wore foxglove blooms on their toes to muffle the sound of their approach as they crept up on their prey.

However, its medicinal uses are even more potent. Used for centuries as a remedy for headaches, in the late eighteenth century the doctor and botanist Dr William Withering became interested in the foxglove as a treatment for dropsy, following an account by 'Old Mother Hutton', a village woman from Shropshire. Now called oedema or fluid retention, at the time dropsy was a common symptom of heart failure. After researching its uses for over nine years, Withering developed digitalis, a drug derived from dried foxglove leaves, which proved to be an important

treatment for heart problems. This was one of the first cases where a traditional herbal remedy was developed into modern medicine, and by the 1920s digitalis was being commercially manufactured by pharmaceutical company Parke-Davis (now part of Pfizer).

Since then, the drug has been used to help control chaotic heart contractions and irregular heart rates. Although some may remember the villain, Le Chiffre, trying to kill James Bond in the 2006 film *Casino Royale* by slipping digitalis into his martini, the risk of dying from foxglove poisoning is very low and not as fast-acting as that action sequence may have led us to believe.

As a country, we seem to have a thing for foxgloves. They're much loved, even chosen as the county flower in Leicestershire, Monmouthshire and Argyll. Between June and September, you can see their purple-pink (and occasionally white) blooms in most places across the country, from roadside verges to hedgerows and creeping into gardens.

And with one plant producing as many as a million seeds, they can easily smother some areas in their biennial blooms.

If you find a patch, don't hurry past. Watch the bumblebees as they push their furry bodies into the mouths of the open flowers, covering themselves with pollen, before flying to another plant to complete their accidental pollination duties. Look out for the mottled brown caterpillars of the foxglove pug moth who fatten up on their flowers, and the lesser yellow underwing moth caterpillars crawling across the leaves.

Whether you know them as 'goblin gloves', 'dragon's mouth', 'floppy dock', 'tod-tails', 'fairy fingers', 'dragon's mouth' or 'Scotch mercury', for a few weeks each year, let's celebrate the power of the humble, though potent, foxglove.

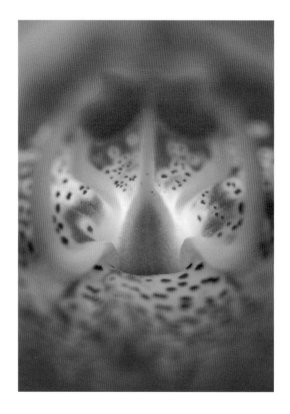

Bats

To watch the flittings of the shrieking bat,
Who, seemly pleas'd to mock our treacherous view,
Would even swoop and touch us as he flew

FROM 'RURAL EVENING' (1820) BY JOHN CLARE

When did you last hear a bat? Quite a while ago if, like me, your childhood years are a distant memory. Bats are unique among mammals in that they use echolocation to navigate and find their food. They click and warble and wait for the sound waves to bounce back to them from their surroundings. As we age, the frequency they use is beyond our adult hearing, but as a child you may have been lucky enough to hear them.

Many people are fearful of bats, which is a shame, as this hasn't always been the case. Before the twentieth century, bats were thought to bring good luck, and local names, such as 'air mouse' and 'flutter mouse', are whimsical rather than frightening. Then in 1897, author Bram Stoker introduced the world to Dracula, an undead monster with a taste for human blood and the ability to transform into a vampire bat. Since then, many books and films have followed suit, and the bat's image has taken a battering.

There are 18 bat species in the UK and some can live for up to 30 years. None are blind. All our native species eat insects and, thankfully, none of them drink our blood; vampire bats are only found in Central and South America. Our bats range from the noctule, our largest bat weighing around 30g (about 1oz), to tiny pipistrelles weighing only a few grams. We also have laws that protect all bats from disturbance and harm.

Natterer's bat

The bat you're most likely to see is the pipistrelle. Every night they will try to catch as many as 3,000 mosquitoes or midges on the wing, often flitting around street lights or zig-zagging over gardens or local parks just after sunset. In the summer months, pipistrelles roost in trees, buildings and bat boxes. In June and July, the females give birth, usually to a single baby known as a pup. The pups are able to fly at three weeks and are fully independent by six weeks. The breeding season will have taken place the previous autumn when the females visit territories defended by the males, but fertilisation does not take place until the following spring, a process known as delayed implantation.

Contrary to what many people believe, bats do not cause damage to property, and if they are living in your house they are just as likely to be hidden away under the cladding or eaves as in the roof space. They don't chew wood, damage wiring or build messy nests, and their droppings are odour-free and dry – in fact you'll hardly notice they are there.

If you want to attract more bats into your local patch, encourage more insects. Moth caterpillars will grow into a tasty meal, so it's good to show some tolerance towards them, even if it's at the expense of a few nibbled leaves. To attract adult moths into your garden, grow highly scented flowers such as jasmine and night-scented stock. Provide some water – even a small bucket pond is beneficial to wildlife and will encourage more insect life. You can even make or buy bat boxes to erect on tree trunks and under eaves. Websites and organisations such as the Bat Conservation Trust provide excellent instructions on how to make bat boxes out of scraps of untreated wood, and where and how you should site them. More than anything, avoid using pesticides in your garden.

As bats fly at night and make no discernible sound, most bats are difficult to identify, but don't let that put you off watching out for them. Their sheer manoeuvrability and speed are unparalleled in the natural world, and you don't need to identify which species they are to appreciate them. Standing in a green space during summer, 20 minutes after sunset, with pipistrelle bats feeding on unseen insects all around you, can be heart-warming, exciting and, let's face it, pretty remarkable. If you want to take your interest in bats to the next level, a heterodyne bat detector makes their echolocation calls audible to older ears.

Breeding season will have taken place the previous autumn when the females visit territories defended by the males, but fertilisation does not take place until the following spring.

Spotted wolf spiders

She's the sprint-specialist of the spider world. A spotted wolf spider. If you listen hard as she scuttles over dead leaves you can hear them rattle; even though she's less than a centimetre long and light as air. Later, you might see her lazing on a stone in the sun surrounded by other lounging wolves, each one with their legs outstretched and ochre bodies pressed against the rock for warmth. You might mistake them for a hunting pack, but this is just a resting place. These wolves do all their hunting alone.

To hunt, you need good eyesight, and the wolf spider's is excellent. Though most spiders have eight eyes (some families have six), many rely on taste, touch and vibrations from their intricate webs to help them 'see'. But the ground-hunting wolf spider has no need for a static web. Instead, it stalks its prey with its two large and four smaller eyes providing superb

forward-facing vision, along with two more eyes on the top and side of its head, that help it see behind and to the side.

Wolf spiders can often be seen hunting in the leaf litter of a wild garden. In spring, don't be in too much of a rush to tidy all the leaves. A thin layer on a flowerbed will act as excellent protection for your plants as well as a hunting ground for invertebrates.

Early in the spring, watch out for the male wolf spider's courtship dance. After finding a likely mate, the much smaller male rears up onto his hind legs and waves his pedipalps – two appendages pre-filled with sperm that look like a pair of boxing gloves – towards the female.

Living a nomadic life has its drawbacks, though. When the female lays her eggs, there's no handy web to use as protection for her young. Instead, she carries her laid eggs with her like a spherical backpack, enclosed in silk and attached to her spinneret, for three to four weeks. This doesn't stop her from hunting; she holds up her abdomen to stop the egg sac from dragging along the ground and carries on.

Her maternal duties don't end once her youngsters hatch. On warm, sunny days in May, keep an eye out for wolf spiders with a moving hairstyle. Look more closely, and you'll see a bouffant of wriggling spiderlings who have climbed onto her back and will stay with her until they are old enough to fend for themselves.

A harmless and fascinating spider to watch, the wolf spider, like all other UK spiders, is vital to our ecosystems. They eat many of the insects we consider a nuisance in our gardens and, in the wider landscape, help to control agricultural pests, reducing the need for pesticides.

If you find it hard to think about – let alone look at – a spider, new medical research might change your mind. Fibroin, one of the key elements in spider silk, has been made into a flexible, strong material and trialled in knee replacements and the healing of broken bones. The silk's

Female spotted wolf spider carrying spiderlings on her back

molecules are so closely aligned to human proteins that our cells can grow into the material. In future, scientists hope the material can be used in hip replacements and even for cartilage discs in the spine.

Researchers have also observed jumping spiders endearingly twitching their legs and moving their eyes rapidly whilst resting. Just like a dog twitches and yelps when dreaming of a chase.

So, if appreciating spiders for their fascinating life cycle isn't your thing, remember they could inspire the next medical breakthrough in heart surgery, fix a severed spine or even further our understanding of sleep.

Chafers

Most often seen in May, you might know them as May beetle or May bug, or for some that appear later in the year (there are several species) June bug, midsummer dor or summer chafer. There are even regional variations, such as 'kittywitch' or 'chovy' in Norfolk, 'billywitch' in Suffolk, and 'chwilen y bwm' in Wales. But in most places, you'll just hear this large, noisy but gentle-giant of a beetle referred to as a cockchafer – Old English for 'big beetle'.

For most of its life – which can be up to five years – the cockchafer lives underground. Adult females lay as many as 80 eggs in the soil in June or July, each of which will hatch into a large, creamy-white larva with a conspicuous light brown head. For several years these larvae will survive on plant and vegetable roots in the soil before pupating and emerging from April onwards as adult beetles.

You can see (or hear) them flying in most areas after sunset, including farmland, woods, urban parks and gardens. They're quite easy to see as they're one of our biggest beetles and can grow to around 3cm (1¼in). The adults only live for five to six weeks above ground, bumbling around, looking for a mate, often flying around oak trees, something that has led to yet another of their common names, the oak-wib. With striking white markings on the sides of their abdomen and a hairy body, the rest of the cockchafer is black except for their brown legs and wing cases.

They don't look like they should be able to fly, but they do, with a loud, disconcerting buzz that has led to more names such as 'humbuz', 'bummler' and 'doodlebug'. The latter was used by London residents as a nickname for German V1 flying bombs during the Second World War because of its similarity to the sound of the cockchafer during flight.

Though cockchafers can't claim to be the most beautiful beetle, their most eye-catching feature is definitely their antennae, which are flattened at the end into a feather-like fan. These olfactory organs not only help them find food, but also to pinpoint a mate. If you get close enough to count each feather, seven will identify it as a male and six as a female.

Their plant-gnawing habits mean they haven't always been a welcome visitor. In 1320, exasperated with the damage cockchafers were causing to their crops, a court in the French town of Avignon ordered the insects to be exiled to a special area of cordoned-off woodland. Unsurprisingly, the beetles didn't comply. Later, in 1574, there are records of cockchafers appearing in such numbers in the Severn Valley that they clogged up the wheels of watermills.

The use of pesticides in the twentieth century very nearly wiped them out but, thankfully, changes to regulations have led to a recovery in their numbers since the 1980s. Today, there are around 20 or so chafer species living in the UK. The common cockchafer *Melolontha melolontha* is the one you're most likely to see, especially if you live in the south of England. There is also the metallic-green rose chafer that, as its name suggests, has a penchant for rose bushes, but many of the other species – such as the noble, variable and bee chafer – are rare.

Rooks and other corvids will eat their larvae, leading to yet another local name, 'rookworm'. Though the number of cockchafers emerging nowadays are unlikely to cause problems for waterwheels, in some bumper years hundreds or even thousands might be seen.

If you're lucky enough to see a large number of cockchafers emerging, watch out for foxes or badgers jumping around and pouncing on them. This can be a much-needed feeding bonanza for a lot of wildlife.

So, on warm spring or summer evenings when you hear the buzzing of a mitchamador, dumbledore or snartlegog, don't be afraid; it's just a harmless chafer flying by.

Male common cockchafer

The smell of earth and summer rain

Of all our senses, smell is perhaps the most under-appreciated. Indeed, as American biologist Rachel Carson says: 'The sense of smell, almost more than any other, has the power to recall memories and it is a pity that we use it so little.' Although perhaps this has now changed. Many of us longed to smell properly again when Covid-19 deprived us of our ability to perceive scents, or altered them so much they became unpleasant. It wasn't just that we couldn't smell food, or that it smelt unappetising, it was the loss of the simple, often unconscious, pleasure of smelling things throughout the day.

The number and quality of the receptors high up in our noses determines the depth, perception and subtlety of the things we smell, and – as with all parts of us – everyone's nose is different. This may go some way to explaining why one person's favourite smell is another's worst, and why scientists have failed to find a smell that is universally disliked for use in riot control. The sense of smell isn't as simple as it might seem.

It also interferes with our memories. Smell receptors have a more direct connection to the regions of our brain processing memory – such as the hippocampus – than any of our other senses. It's no wonder that certain smells, especially those connected to nature and happy memories, can reduce stress.

Though we can't all agree on a smell we dislike, there is one that everyone seems to enjoy. You may not know what it's called, but you know what it smells like. It's the scent of newly turned warm soil, of summer showers splashing against hot paving slabs and the smell of rain on the breeze. It's clean, distinctive, fresh, wild and instantly recognisable.

In the 1960s, two Australian scientists, Isabel (Joy) Bear and Richard Thomas, decided to discover its source. They named it petrichor: 'petra'

(stone) and 'ichor' (ethereal fluid). Hard rain or digging releases the scent by disturbing a compound in the soil called geosmin, which is produced by *Streptomyces* bacteria, the source of many of our most successful antibiotics.

Perhaps we instinctively know it is good for us. Something that could be a throwback to when rain, and the water it brought, was a life-saver. Even now, if you ask someone about their favourite natural scent, they will often say the smell of the earth after summer rain. It's obvious that recognising the smell of petrichor is deep within our human psyche.

So, when it happens, make sure you're ready to appreciate it. Notice the smell that bounces up as the rain beats down on a hot, dry pavement in the middle of a busy town. Take a walk in a woodland in late summer and kick the top layer of leaves so that they release their geosmin elixir.

Though we find smells hard to describe, and often lack the vocabulary to do them justice, wherever you go, whatever your experiences, petrichor can transport you back in time.

Marmalade hoverflies

Most of us can only dream of watching the spectacle of migrating monarch butterflies in California. Yet there's a phenomenon that is just as awe-inspiring and goes almost unnoticed, which happens right here on our doorstep. The star of the show is the marmalade hoverfly: a shiny, small, black-and-orange striped insect, one of hundreds of hoverfly species found in the UK.

Recent research warns that 41 per cent of our insects are hurtling towards extinction because of habitat loss, the climate crisis and an increased use of pesticides. Of those, a quarter could disappear in the next 10 years. These are frightening predictions as insects are beneficial in so many ways, from food for animals and pollinating crops, to keeping our ecosystems running smoothly. Yet our feelings towards them are often ambivalent, or worse, negative. A dislike of flies and wasps can even bring out our killer instinct.

Though all insects are important, marmalade hoverflies are especially amazing. More than any other fly, they deserve our respect and admiration. Each spring, some 700 million marmalade hoverflies migrate to the UK from Europe, navigating vast expanses of water and land. Arriving as they do in such huge numbers, they are often spotted on radars. Once here, they feed on the nectar of flowers and are second only to bees in the help they provide – for free – towards commercial crop and fruit pollination.

That said, these newly arrived adults only live for around a month. But before they die, they provide yet another beneficial service. On finding a group of aphids, each female marmalade hoverfly will lay hundreds of eggs which, once hatched into larvae, will eat up to 300 aphids a day. That's six trillion aphids consumed, representing a huge biological

Each spring, some 700 million marmalade hoverflies migrate to the UK from Europe, navigating vast expanses of water and land.

contribution to pest control for our farmers.

Though they might appear wasp-like in their stripy coats, they are, like all species of hoverfly, harmless to humans. Their appearance protects them from their adversaries who wrongly assume they can sting – something known as Batesian mimicry. Larvae that develop in hot temperatures can turn into vibrant orange adults, but in cooler temperatures, some adults that emerge are nearly black. If you want to tell the difference between males and females, look for their large, dark red compound eyes. If they touch at the top, it's a male; if they don't, it's a female.

Unlike other insects, numbers of marmalade hoverflies have bucked insect decline trends, and have remained relatively stable. During any year, up to four billion of them can be flying around over southern Britain. You'll find them just about everywhere, from arable fields and wetlands, to gardens and inner-city parks. Any flower – if there is easy access to pollen and nectar – will be popular. Plus, you can see them in any month of the year, even mid-winter. They tuck themselves away during the colder months but can wake from dormancy on warm winter days to feed.

At the height of summer, over a billion marmalade hoverflies prepare to leave. This is when you can experience an amazing spectacle as they gather along our coasts. Generations upon generations of hoverflies, descended from those initial spring migrants, now glitter like orange-black jewels, dotting every flower, every leaf, every bare surface. Here they'll stay, gentle and harmless, waiting for the favourable winds that will help them on their journey to continental Europe.

Moles

With its long inquisitive nose, cylindrical body and short stocky legs, you could say the mole is like a small hedgehog, minus the spines, of course. Both eat copious quantities of worms, are cute and rarely seen. But there's one big difference: we have a huge soft spot for hedgehogs but are unashamedly hostile towards moles.

Ever since humans first cultivated the land, we've had a difficult relationship with these mysterious creatures. The mole was once a woodland animal, feasting on the rich, worm-filled loam beneath the trees, but as we cleared its habitat, it moved out into the cultivated landscape.

Even though they're a common mammal, we know surprisingly little about them. Once called moldwarp or mouldywarp, meaning 'the one that throws soil', males and females dig a complex of permanent and temporary tunnels with their outward-facing front claws; swimming breaststroke through the soil. Their tunnels can be hundreds of metres long and several metres deep, and they act as ingenious food traps for insects, larvae and earthworms that the patrolling mole sometimes stores in specially built food chambers.

As moles spend most of their time in the dark, they are thought to be colour blind and near-sighted but can still detect light. Being underground also reduces their need for good hearing. Instead of external ears, they feel vibrations and have an excellent sense of smell.

Though they eat a similar diet, they're much smaller than hedgehogs. An average mole is about 15cm (6in) long, weighs about 80g (3oz), and needs to eat at least 50g (1¾oz) of earthworms a day to survive. It feeds and sleeps in a shift pattern of a few hours on and a few hours off, in total darkness, all year round.

If you're wondering how moles breathe below ground, it's thought our European mole has the same ingenious adaptation as the Eastern mole (found in North America and Canada) – special haemoglobin in its blood that allows it to carry more carbon dioxide, and therefore rebreathe its own air.

Moles live for a couple of years and though their population in the UK (they are absent from Ireland) is thought to be around 35–40 million, there have been signs that since 2000 this might be declining.

This is nothing new: in the nineteenth century, moles were killed to satisfy the demand for moleskin clothing. Though this fashion faded, vast numbers continued to be killed each year in spring traps or with poison.

Farmers maintain that earth from molehills taints harvested silage and causes damage to farm machinery, and that the mole's underground tunnels disturb the growth of crops and cause problems with drainage. It doesn't stop there. In more urban areas, on the pristine grass of golf courses, cricket pitches, racecourses and parks, their digging has brought moles into conflict with greenkeepers and grounds people. It's a yearly cull that continues unnoticed, though this probably does little to affect their overall numbers.

The most likely time to see a mole is when males come above ground to look for a mate in early spring, when they are collecting nesting material, during droughts and when the young separate from their mothers at around five or six weeks of age. In February 2022, a mole even wandered into a shop in Stowmarket, though how it got there, no one is quite sure. You're more likely to see one if you find a molehill that is regularly topped up with fresh soil. A stakeout might lead to a rare mole sighting as it pops its head above ground.

On the plus side, moles can be useful in gardens, as they eat pests and aerate the soil (molehill soil apparently makes the best potting compost). For a little unevenness in your lawn and the odd molehill, perhaps we can be more tolerant of this much-maligned and misunderstood mammal.

Controversially, moles can be useful in gardens, as they eat pests and aerate the soil (molehill soil apparently makes the best potting compost).

Flying ants

Who hasn't, at one time or another, found ants annoying? They overrun our homes, crawl on us, eat our food at picnics, some of them even bite. Then, to top it off, and for no apparent reason, they swarm in colossal numbers in the middle of a summer's day when we want to be outside. After all that, it's probably safe to assume most of us aren't massive fans. But we should be. Ants are not so different from us.

There's thought to be over a quadrillion (that's a million billion) ants in the world. Even though their colonies are founded by a queen, they have no overall leader. Like humans, they live in close-knit communities, where their collective decisions benefit their entire colony. The queen is an egg-laying machine. Most of her eggs will develop into female workers, who will start their lives looking after the queen, tending to new eggs and larvae, before progressing to waste disposal, foraging for food and handling conflicts. Some of the queen's eggs, later in the year, will also develop into new queens and males. You could say the ant's caste system is just about as democratic as it gets.

In the UK, the species we most often encounter is the black garden ant, *Lasius niger*. In individual colonies of between four and seven thousand, these ants nest unseen beneath our garden paving slabs and lawns, spending their entire lives unknowingly (and very helpfully) pollinating our garden plants, acting as pest control and dispersing seeds.

Then, on a warm, humid summer's day, they suddenly become very visible. In July 2020, the Met Office's weather radar detected a cloud 80km (50 miles) wide, which made its way over the south-east of England. But this was no rain cloud: it was a swarm of mating flying ants. When conditions are right, winged virgin queens and smaller-winged males burst from their nests and climb as high as they can up grass and

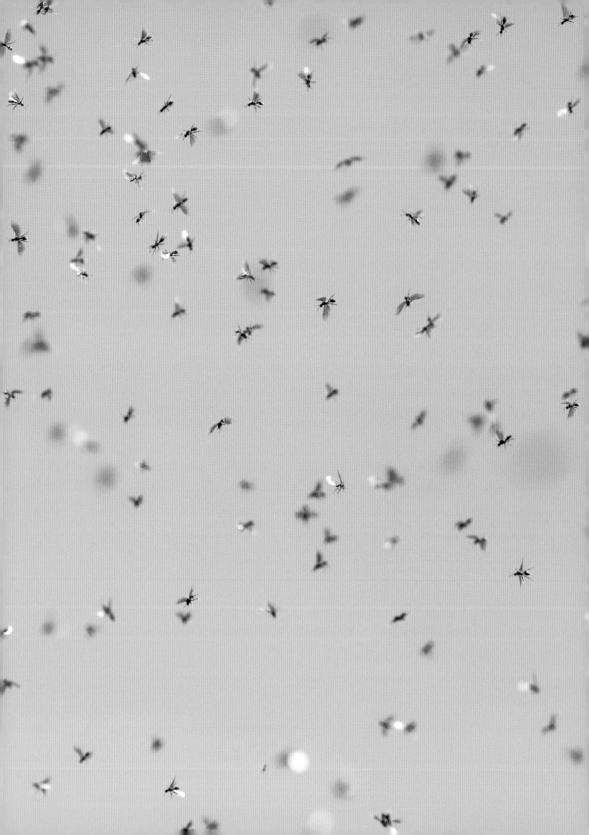

plant stems and take to the air. Other local colonies, encouraged by the same good weather, swarm as well. This allows thousands of queens and males to mix and mate on the wing, and if you see birds above your garden, such as gulls, swallows and swifts, they could be taking advantage of a free invertebrate meal.

Though the males die within a week, for the young mated queens, life is just beginning. Once they have dropped to the ground and shed their wings, they will start their own nests. These queens are one of our most long-lived insects, often surviving up to 15 years, and will never need to mate again. The sperm they collected on their nuptial flight will fertilise their eggs for the rest of their lives.

No wonder many scientists believe ants, not humans, are the pinnacle of social intelligence.

Though small, the collective organisation of ants is impressive. Scientists at Bristol University have been studying how ants solve complex problems. They found forager worker ants that had purposely been infected with a microscopic fungus socially distanced themselves from other ants. They also witnessed other ants behaving in a similar way, even though they weren't infected, thereby decreasing the risk of infection to the entire colony.

No wonder many scientists believe ants, not humans, are the pinnacle of social intelligence. Something to remember the next time one wanders into your kitchen, or you see swarming ants on a summer's day.

Ladybirds

The name 'ladybird' has been used for over 600 years; it alludes to the Virgin Mary (Our Lady), draped in a red cloak. This little flying insect is undoubtedly one of our most easily recognised beetles. Or is it? Of the 47 species in the UK, only 26 are what experts term 'conspicuous' and resemble the insect of which we are so fond. As children, it is exciting to see a ladybird's shiny wings open as it prepares to take flight, and we all learn the rhyme:

Ladybird, ladybird fly away home.
Your house is on fire, and your children are gone,
All except one, and her name is Ann,
And she hid under the baking pan.

The cute, rotund, short-legged and frequently spotty character we associate with the name is, in fact, the adult phase of the ladybird's lifecycle. Their younger – and some say uglier – alter-egos often go unrecognised, or are sometimes misidentified as pests, which a ladybird most definitely is not. They are a gardener's and farmer's friend: one seven-spot ladybird can lay a thousand eggs and eat over 5,000 aphids during its lifetime. If you encourage a healthy population of ladybirds into your garden you could reduce problems caused by destructive aphids.

Ladybird larvae go through distinct stages during their lives. Tiny when first hatched, their larva soon grow and moult, not once but four times, becoming progressively easier to identify with each reincarnation. They live on aphids and other tiny pest insects, and with their spiked bodies and six stumpy legs are easily mistaken for caterpillars.

Just as adult ladybird species look different from one another, their young are the same. The seven-spot ladybird's third and fourth instar (the period between moults) is a grey-black colour with four pairs of orange blotches on its body, while the orange ladybird is yellow and black between moults. However, within a few weeks, they will pupate and then hatch as adults, ready to start the cycle all over again the next spring.

The ladybird's penchant for aphids has even led to the non-native Asian harlequin ladybird being introduced as a commercial pest control method in the USA and elsewhere. It was good at pest control. Too good. It has since spread into the wild and is now threatening to out-compete native ladybirds, not only in the United States but also in South America, Europe and parts of Africa. Long term, it's hoped that UK farmers can help native populations by encouraging them into aphid-affected crops naturally.

We can do the same. By growing plants that attract aphids, such as roses and some vegetables, you can often attract more native ladybirds into your garden. Plus, planting companion plants, such as calendula and marigold, in or near to your veg patch often boosts the numbers of ladybirds who can deal with any aphid problems.

You could also provide adult ladybirds with places to hide. Log piles and insect refuges, filled with sticks and fur cones, make perfect places for them to overwinter.

It's difficult to say how our native ladybirds will fare in the future. Ladybirds might disappear from areas that do not provide for their needs. Why the ladybird's house was on fire and Ann was hiding under the baking pan may always remain a mystery, but hopefully, they won't fly away soon. Especially as the more ladybirds we can encourage, the healthier our garden ecosystems will stay.

Seven-spot ladybird larva

Beadlet sea anemones

'The flower of the sea'. If you spend some time at the seaside, one creature you're likely to encounter is the sea anemone. Though there are more than 70 species in the UK, their botanical names and appearances can be deceptive. This is an animal, rather than a plant, and is more closely related to corals and jellyfish than seaweed. With names like strawberry, dahlia, daisy and snakelock, the anemones found in our waters are recognised as some of the most beautiful in the world.

One of the easiest to identify, and one of the most common on rocky shores, is the beadlet anemone. When the tide is out, it takes on the appearance of a blob of red or orange-green jelly. However, as the water returns, finger-like tentacles emerge surrounding a central mouth. These tentacles contain nematocysts, stinging cells that, when triggered, fire venom-filled filaments into small fish or prawns. This is a mechanism that's thought to be one of the fastest and most complex in the whole of the animal kingdom. A ring of blue beads around the base of the anemone's body gives it its common name. These blue acrorhagi are used to sting other anemones but are harmless to humans.

In a quirk of evolution, young beadlet anemones are produced without the need for sexual reproduction. After being brooded inside the adult's body cavity, the young are expelled from the mouth as fully formed miniature clones that can live independently straight away.

Although beadlet anemones often stay in one position for weeks at a time, they can still move if they need to. Their basal disc, which keeps them secure, can move them infinitesimally slowly across rocks or, if they need to escape from predators, they can detach themselves and let the sea currents move them to a new location.

Anemones have also developed strange relationships with other organisms. In the famous Pixar animation, *Finding Nemo*, the clownfish may have found shelter within the tentacles of an anemone, but here in the UK anemones have buddied up with algae. Found in the tentacles of snakelock anemone, zooxanthellae (a dinoflagellate alga) supplies its anemone host with oxygen and sugars during photosynthesis. In return, the snakelock protects the algae from being eaten by small fish and crustaceans. It's a win-win situation.

Beadlet anemones can live for an incredibly long time. Successive owners kept a particular specimen, which was given the name Granny, for 59 years. It had been taken from a Scottish shoreline in 1828 and kept in a glass jar. The anemone became quite a celebrity during its lifetime, to the extent that when it died just before Queen Victoria's Golden Jubilee, those caring for Granny feared the news would cause widespread mourning, so it was delayed until after the celebrations.

This is an animal, rather than a plant, and is more closely related to corals and jellyfish than seaweed.

Nowadays, we all appreciate that it's better to leave wildlife in the wild. However, with pollution and siltation affecting much of our coastline, our marine wildlife needs all the help and protection it can get.

The next time you stare into a rock pool and marvel at the extraordinary creatures that live within it, think of this fragile habitat not as a holiday amusement but as an underwater nature reserve and learn about the best ways to protect it.

Dragonflies and damselflies

It's hard not to admire dragonflies. The way their iridescent gauzy wings catch the light on a summer's day or the flash of metallic blue or green as they sweep across a lake. They take your breath away. In 'The Two Voices' Alfred, Lord Tennyson, described his impression of the dragonfly:

He dried his wings: like gauze they grew;
Thro' crofts and pastures wet with dew
A living flash of light he flew.

Whereas nature books and articles have concentrated on pollinators such as butterflies and bees, not as much has been written about dragonflies, which is a shame. This enigmatic insect is a good news story, at a time when we need all the good news about nature we can get.

Of the 46 species of dragonfly and damselfly that live or migrate to Britain and Ireland, over 40 per cent have increased in number during the last 50 years. Helped by rising temperatures, wetland habitat restoration and cleaner waterways, the fact that they are doing so well feels like something we should be celebrating.

In Japan, dragonflies are revered as symbols of courage and strength, but in the UK they don't seem to share the same status. Here they were known as 'horse-stingers' – erroneously, of course, as dragonflies do not sting. Another name, 'devil's darning needles', seems to stem from a myth that damselflies, with their long, needle-like bodies, could sew your eyelids shut if you dared to snooze by a river. No doubt this was a useful way of discouraging lazy farmworkers from a daytime nap.

We tend to bunch all the species together as dragonflies, in what's known as the order Odonata (meaning 'toothed jaw' because of their serrated mouthparts), but they actually fall into two separate groups: dragonflies and damselflies.

Dragonflies are large, strong flyers and can often be spotted hunting for prey away from water. Like all Odonata, they have four wings, and their hind wings are usually broader and slightly shorter than the forewings. Their large compound eyes usually touch at the top and, when they land, they generally hold their wings at 90 degrees to their body.

Damselflies are smaller and daintier. All four of their wings are a similar size and shape, and they're quite weak flyers. They prefer to stay close to water and, unlike dragonflies, their smaller eyes never touch.

Blue-tailed damselfly

Although some can grow quite large (the emperor dragonfly has a wingspan of up to 12cm or 4¾in), neither dragonflies nor damselflies can bite or sting us, though they are ferocious predators of small flies and other insects.

Their lifecycle is long and complex. It begins with laying their eggs slightly above or below water. Once hatched, their larvae resemble wingless mini-monsters and prey on freshwater invertebrates living underwater. The larvae moult between five and 14 times before emerging – sometimes years later – as adults.

Once out of the water, they reorganise their body fluids and push themselves out of their larval skin; then wait for their body and wings to harden before taking their first tentative and weak flights. Now their imperative is to mate and lay eggs, after which they'll only live a few more weeks.

Though you might think the chance of seeing a dragonfly or damselfly in your garden is unlikely, they are actually fairly easy to encourage. If your garden is full of insects, and you make room for a pond (even a small one), it won't be long before you'll see them darting across your flowerbeds and dancing, locked together with their mate.

Their method of flight has also inspired scientists. Impressed by the dragonfly's aerial skills, they have developed drones that flap like a dragonfly. Unlike fixed wings, these flapping drones reduce drag and even increase the amount that can be carried. Who knows, in the future giant dragonfly drones could be delivering your parcels.

Though most dragonflies are climate change survivors, we still need to be vigilant. Five of the UK's dragonfly and damselfly species have declined, some pushed to the margins of their more northerly habitats. Even dragons aren't beyond the negative impacts of humankind.

Four-spotted chaser dragonfly

The elder and its berries

The elder is a tree that most people have heard of; it is even mentioned in the film *Monty Python and the Holy Grail* in the immortal line, 'Your mother was a hamster and your father smelt of elderberries!' But for most of the year it goes under the radar. It's well-suited to our climate and is a stubbornly successful plant. From railway sidings to parks, hedges to brownfield sites, it grows nearly anywhere. The elder's wrinkled, grey-brown bark, short trunk and multiple stems may go unnoticed, but it has long been important in folklore and as a herbal medicine and a culinary ingredient.

In the past, we seemed to appreciate and care for our native trees much more than we do today. The elder tree was used to make dye: black from its bark; yellow and green from its leaves; blue and purple from its berries. We used its hollow, fast-growing stems as bellows to add strength (air) to our fires. In the Greco-Roman world, the wood was used to make a musical instrument, a sambuca, no doubt contributing to the plant's Latin name, *Sambucus nigra*.

As well as being a useful and important tree to humans, it is also surrounded with myths and legends. Elder is thought to come from the Anglo-Saxon word, *aeld*, meaning 'fire', and legend has it that you would be cursed if you burned its wood. If you planted an elder close to your home, it was supposed to give you protection from witches and lightning. Witches were also thought to turn themselves into elder trees by gathering beneath its leaves. The Earth Mother – a female spirit or goddess who was the giver of life – was also thought to live within the elder's branches. People would never take anything from the tree without first asking the Earth Mother's permission.

The elder's frothy white flowers put on a striking show in spring. As well as being useful for pollinating insects, they also make a deliciously sweet cordial. But it's between August and October when the blue-black berries ripen that they become popular as an ingredient in wines, syrups and preserves. However, be warned: if eaten raw, elderberries are eye-wateringly sour and only lose their toxicity if you cook or ferment them. High in vitamin C and antioxidants, their syrup is also said to soothe a sore throat.

Elderberries have a luscious berry smell – most people would be happy to smell of elderberries – but its leaves are a different matter. Their scent is extremely unpleasant, especially if bruised. In days gone by, branches and leafy twigs would be hung outside dairies, fixed onto horses'

The elder's wrinkled, grey-brown bark, short trunk and multiple stems may go unnoticed, but it has long been important in folklore and as a herbal medicine and a culinary ingredient.

bridles, and poked into the brims of fishermen's hats to ward off flies. It's now known that its leaves produce cyanide when crushed.

Before foraging the flowers or berries for yourself, give a thought to other creatures that might need the elder more. In early autumn, white-spotted pug and buff ermine caterpillars both feed on its foliage. Robins and blackbirds, and mammals such as dormice and bank voles, will often eat elderberries. If you find a tree in full fruit, be mindful of what you take, and leave plenty for hungry wildlife.

Late-summer dew

You realise the season is changing when the dew grows heavy. Grass that turned yellow and dry over the summer now starts each morning as a silvered lake of dew. Daytime temperatures still top 20ºC (68ºF), and the leaves cling firmly to trees, but the days are noticeably shorter. Clear, windless nights are cool. The ground is losing its heat. It won't be long before autumn is here.

Of course, dew isn't fussy where it forms. Windows that have retained their daytime heat but then cool overnight also encourage airborne water vapour to condense. Suddenly it's a lot harder to see out of the windows first thing in the morning, which is a clear sign that change is happening.

Although there's a somewhat melancholic beauty to this time of year, it's also a time of celebration. In rural England, 24 August, or St Bartholomew's Day, was not only believed to bring the first dews but also herald the start of many fairs and festivals.

In folklore, dew was regarded as a remedy for aches, pains and skin conditions. People would make a point of walking through dew barefoot to get the most benefit from its healing powers. Some would even go as far as rolling around in it naked.

Wildlife also notice these subtle seasonal changes. If you've ever been lucky enough to see a field criss-crossed in spider silk, sparkling with dew, it's probably the remnants of a mass spider exodus.

As summer comes to an end, money spiders take to the sky. Without wings to help them colonise new territories and move away from their parents and siblings, spiderlings climb nearby

As their gossamer threads solidify, an army of spiderlings is lifted into the sky.

grass stems, and en masse, point their abdomens to the clouds and pull silken strands from their spinnerets. As their gossamer threads solidify, an army of spiderlings is lifted into the sky.

Known as ballooning, but more reminiscent of kite flying, these glistening threads may carry the tiny spiderling a few metres or many thousands of kilometres. The spider has no control and though it was presumed that the wind was lifting them, research has found electrical fields in the atmosphere provide an extra boost.

Don't miss the late summer dew. If there's still strength in the sun, its glistening beauty will be gone before lunchtime. There's something magical about being the first to walk across a dew-laden meadow, looking behind at pristine footprints in a silver sea.

Go the whole hog as our ancestors did. Go barefoot. Feel the shock of the cold, the softness of the grass, the trickle of pure water on your skin. Look in detail at the way dew forms on the foliage around you, how it pools in the centre of leaves, causing hairs and veins to be magnified. Notice how the dew turns a dandelion clock into a glass globe or catches the light like a teardrop hanging at the end of a petal. Smell the air. Even in a town or city, a heavy dew can clear the dust and dirt of summer.

Catch it before it goes. Autumn is nearly here.

Orb-weaver spider

AUTUMN

Grasshoppers and crickets

In October, as we cling to the fading summer days and shudder at the chilly nights of autumn taking hold, the common field grasshopper is entering the most significant and final few weeks of its life.

Back in early spring, the grasshopper emerged as a nymph from eggs laid the previous year. Over the spring and summer, it fed on grass and moulted up to five times. On reaching maturity in the autumn it would have mated and, if it was a female, laid eggs – the eggs that will become next summer's grasshopper population.

If, over the last few years, you've planted your own wildflower area or let your lawn grow long, you may already have resident grasshoppers. They might hop out of the way as you cross their path or jump off plants while you're pruning. Though we are most likely to see grasshoppers during hot, dry summer spells, early autumn is the best time to appreciate this armour-plated insect's beauty and behaviour.

There's no rushing a grasshopper encounter. You could say they're the ideal antidote to a hectic lifestyle, as you need a sunny day and plenty of time to dawdle. If you have both, then find a quiet spot in a grassy meadow, field or wildlife-friendly garden in early October, and settle down to wait. Watch as the grass sways in the breeze and appreciate the last vestiges of autumn warmth.

Eventually, a grasshopper may appear, crawling through the blades, stopping occasionally for a munch or two of grass. If it's a male, it might still be calling for potential mates by stridulating – the noise it makes by scraping its long back legs against its wings like a violin. Or you may see a female pushing her sharp ovipositor, or egg tube, into the ground to lay her eggs.

In the UK, there are 11 grasshopper and 16 native cricket species.

Great green bush-cricket

Although both grasshoppers and crickets have six legs, two pairs of wings (although some can't fly), five eyes and prefer warm temperatures, there are some noticeable differences that can be useful if you're trying to tell them apart.

Crickets are more active at dusk or during the night, and their antennae are usually longer than their bodies. Most rub their wings together to sing, although the oak bush-cricket stamps its feet on leaves.

Grasshoppers, on the other hand, are most active during the day. They have much shorter antennae and they 'sing' as described above. If you can get really close, you'll be able to inspect their five eyes: two larger compound eyes for vision, and three smaller, simpler eyes to perceive changes in light intensity.

Though you wouldn't guess it, physiologically grasshoppers are remarkably like us. So much so in fact that research into the way their cells divide has been used to detect substances our bodies might find carcinogenic.

There is also a debate over whether grasshoppers should become a staple of British diets. They could prove to be a more sustainable and environmentally friendly alternative to livestock farming as they take up less land, need less food and produce fewer emissions. Insects have been eaten in Africa and Asia for thousands of years, and they're also an excellent source of nutrients, including iron, protein, calcium and vitamins. Though whether dried grasshoppers will become commonplace in local supermarkets remains to be seen.

Common field grasshopper

Autumn bounty

Waiting for autumn's wild bounty can feel like waiting for a bus. You watch all year as wild fruits and nuts develop, then they all seem to ripen at the same time. The landscape is overflowing.

Trying to unpick the nomenclature of our native nuts and fruits can prove frustrating. There are nuts that are fruits. Some fruits are pomes or haws. There are even some berry-like fruits known as drupes. They all look good enough to eat, but what if you aren't 100 per cent sure what they are, or whether you should pick them?

Encased in their own protective wrapper, they contain everything required for a plant to grow. As the seeds expand and swell, they develop into that catch-all term, fruit.

Nuts are a dry, single-seeded fruit, usually with a hard or leathery husk. They develop from the enlarged and hardened ovary wall of the

Conker from a horse chestnut tree

Song thrush feeding on sloes (blackthorn)

fertilised flower. In the UK, true nuts include conkers (from horse chestnut), hazelnuts (from hazel) and acorns (from oak).

Then there are the drupes. These are fruits where the seed develops within a hard coating, surrounded by a fleshy layer and outer skin. In the wild, these include sloes (blackthorn) and damsons – the latter being brought to the UK by the Romans. Though drupes are very tart when raw, they can be cooked and used to make lovely jams and preserves, but they're especially beneficial for winter migratory birds, such as fieldfares, fattening up for the winter.

When is a nut, not a nut? When it's a walnut. Protected by three fleshy layers of husk, the walnut is one of a few culinary nuts that are actually drupes, or drupaceous nuts. This is likely to be another Roman introduction, as they were especially fond of walnuts. As well as a tasty seed, the outer husks were used to produce fabric dyes, hair dyes and inks. The seeds are ready to harvest when their green outer casing splits open either on or off the tree, usually around October.

Harvest mouse on rose hips

Fruits such as rowan, crab apple and hawthorn are classified as pomes. These come from the same family as cultivated apples and pears that have a tough central core. And just to confuse matters, the single-seeded haws of hawthorn are sometimes also classed as a drupe.

Prized for their high vitamin C content, the bright red rose hips of native wild roses are an accessory or false succulent fruit, where a fruit develops from parts of the flower other than the ovary. Their fleshy covering is lined with hairs that are itchy if they come into contact with human skin and should be removed to make rose hip syrup or jams, but birds such as blackbirds and song thrushes don't seem to be affected.

Should you collect this glorious bounty to make food for yourself? If you live in the countryside and the local harvest is large, you probably can. But if the harvest in your local area already seems small, it's better to leave them for wildlife. For a dormouse or a newly arrived fieldfare, a fallen crab apple or a delicious rose hip could mean the difference between life and death.

Ivy and the last of the insects

As winter draws closer, it can feel as if we're saying goodbye to the insects. Since spring, they've pollinated our veggies and filled our gardens with their soporific buzz and flutter. Then things start to change. There's a nip in the air. Days get shorter, and flowers turn to seed. Don't worry, it's not quite the end. Many insects will still be around, they've just decamped to the ivy flowers.

Do the ivy's aerial rooted stems make you nervous? It can be a pushy plant, even a bit of a thug, but opinions are slowly changing. In the ecological community, it's no longer frowned on for damaging trees or brickwork with its roots. Instead, ivy is now recognised as so important to late-season insects that Francis Ratnieks, Professor of Apiculture at the University of Sussex, has claimed that if it didn't exist, we would probably have tried to invent it.

If you walk anywhere during September or October, in towns, cities or the countryside, you are likely to smell an unusual honey scent. Not everyone likes it and you may even have walked straight past. But next time you become aware of it, look around and find the source; as you get nearer, you'll hear the buzzing of hundreds of insects, feasting on ivy's autumn banquet.

The flowers only bloom once the parent plant is more than 10 years old. Perhaps that is why we don't see the flowers in our gardens, as many of us remove ivy before it reaches this age. Left to mature, its pointed leaves turn oval, and its stems become woodier

> *Ivy is now recognised as so important to late-season insects that one scientist has claimed that if it didn't exist, we would probably have tried to invent it.*

and self-supporting. In late August – in a sunny, light position – it will bloom. The unusual flowers resemble lime green balls that gradually develop into mini fireworks waiting to explode. A single mature ivy plant produces hundreds – if not thousands – of pale yellow and green blooms, silhouetted against a background of the darkest green leaves. No wonder insects make a bee-line for them.

It turns out our nemesis is a bit of an all-round wonder plant for wildlife. As many as 15 or more species of bird feed on ivy's winter berries, and nest within its stems. Insects hibernate within its protective foliage, and it's the food of choice for at least nine species of butterfly and moth caterpillar, including the holly blue butterfly and swallow-tailed moth.

But it's the 30 species of hoverfly, as well as honeybees, butterflies, bumblebees, wasps and aptly named ivy bees, who feast on its autumn nectar and pollen that propel it into superstar status.

You'll never forget the first time you stand in front of an imposing stand of flowering ivy. With insects flying centimetres from your nose, the noise alone is enough to send a fizz of excitement down your spine. Don't worry about the insects. They won't bother you. They're far too engrossed in collecting the last of the year's nectar and pollen. Close your eyes for a moment and absorb the sound. Imagine what it's like to be a smartly striped ivy bee, fresh from its nest, collecting pollen for its young, or a red admiral butterfly plunging its tongue into the sugary nectar, building up reserves to see it through winter hibernation. Whether its smell is one that you love or loathe, ivy is a plant to be celebrated.

Galls

Resembling miniature spaceships, buttons, marbles or pincushions, autumn is the perfect time to spot galls. Over a thousand have been recorded in the UK, and they're most easily described as an abnormal growth. Usually found on fungi and plants, galls are commonly caused by insects, but can be triggered by viruses, fungi or bacteria. Each type of gall has a clever way to manipulate its host to provide it with food, shelter and protection, and although this is a one-way relationship, the host doesn't tend to be harmed. You could call galls quirky shelters for squatters.

The best thing about galls is that they are easy to find. A close look at some of our most common trees and plants should lead to some interesting finds.

First, look at the underside of oak leaves, either fallen or still on the tree. Common spangle galls look like tiny, alien spacecraft

Each type of gall has a clever way to manipulate its host to provide it with food, shelter and protection.

about 5mm (¼in) across. During summer, the wasp *Neuroterus quercusbaccarum* lays its eggs in the top layer of leaf cells, which causes a protective gall to grow around its developing larvae. Eventually, the gall will fall to the ground, and the developing grubs inside will hatch as adults the following spring.

Another tiny wasp, *Andricus kollari*, causes marble galls. Eggs laid by the wasps in the buds of oak trees in late spring produce chemicals that cause a marble-like gall to grow. Each is home to a larva that will emerge as an adult wasp from August onwards. If you find a hole in a brown marble gall in autumn, this is a telltale sign that its tenant has already left. Very similar to marble galls, but caused by a different species of wasp, are oak apple galls. For centuries, both galls were used in the production of iron gall ink. This water-resistant and permanent ink was used by Leonardo da Vinci and the scholars of the Dead Sea scrolls.

The bedeguar gall, from *bād-āwar*, a Persian word meaning 'wind-brought', is a strange, hairy but common gall, found on the stems of several varieties of roses. It starts off green and turns red in the autumn. Also known as 'Robin's pincushion', this name is thought to derive from Robin Goodfellow, a sprite in English folklore who may or may not have used it to store his pins. The wasp, *Diplolepis rosae*, lays several dozen eggs within the bud tissue of the rose and once hatched, the larvae live on the tissue within the gall, pupate over winter and emerge in spring as adult wasps. The bedeguar gall was traditionally used in remedies; hung around the neck as a treatment for whooping cough and placed in the pocket to help rheumatism. A gall placed under a pillow was thought to be a cure for insomnia, but if it wasn't removed, it was said you might never wake.

Another gall – ergot – is a little different. Caused by a fungus, *Claviceps purpurea*, it affects the seeds of grasses such as false oats and rye.

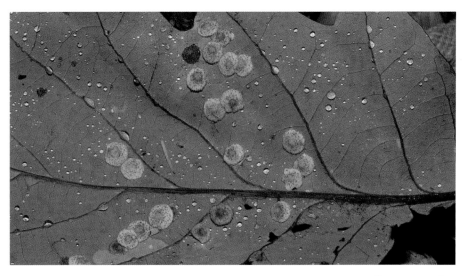

Common spangle

When used in bread-making, the infected rye would cause widespread illness and hallucinations. In medieval times this condition was known as St Anthony's Fire (after the saint of the same name who was sent terrifying visions by the devil), and the illness was treated in specialist hospitals in Europe, set up by the Order of St Anthony. Unsurprisingly, the primary treatment was to stop eating infected bread. However, ergot does have some medicinal uses. Historically, it was used to induce abortions and to stop bleeding during childbirth, and more recently, medicines derived from this gall have been used in the treatment of Parkinson's disease, migraines and non-cancerous tumours of the pituitary gland.

How galls, and what produces them, are able to rearrange cells and manipulate tissue to create these oddities is still largely a mystery, but just finding a gall can open your eyes to a whole other niche of our natural world.

Robin's pincushion

Oak apple gall

Deer rut

We've lived with them for thousands of years. From Derby – the village of the deer – to Hindhead – the hill frequented by hinds – this is an animal ingrained in our culture, mythology, folklore and language. We've hunted them for their meat and skins, artists have painted them, and poets have written about them. What is it about them that is so beguiling?

In autumn, the haunting bellows and clashes of deer antler are often enough to make your heart beat faster and raise the hairs on the back of your neck, not in fear, but excitement at your proximity to something so wild.

We rarely encounter such wildness in our domesticated, twenty-first century lives. Yet deer display its very essence, especially during the rut. Testosterone-pumped males and receptive females are dragged together by their natural instincts. It's a dangerous time. Not just for stags that may fight to the death, but also for humans that might venture too close.

Six deer are found in the UK. The red, fallow, sika and much smaller Chinese water deer all rut in the autumn. Roe deer mate in July and August, while Reeves's muntjac deer mate all year round. Of those that mate in the autumn, only red deer are truly native to the UK. They are widespread in Scotland, England and Northern Ireland, and are also our largest wild land mammal.

Originally, fallow deer were brought to the UK from the western Mediterranean by the Romans and kept in enclosures. However, they died out, but were later re-introduced by the Normans in the eleventh century. Fallow deer are now found across Wales and England, with a patchier distribution in Northern Ireland and Scotland.

Japanese sika deer are also widespread in Scotland, but less so in

Red deer (stag)

*We rarely encounter such wildness
in our domesticated, twenty-first century
lives. Yet deer display its very essence,
especially during the rut.*

England and Northern Ireland. Chinese water deer are escapees from captive herds brought to the UK in the 1860s and '70s. As their name suggests, they prefer wet habitats, and this small, tusked deer lives feral in Bedfordshire and the fenlands of Cambridgeshire and Norfolk.

If you want to experience the autumn deer rut, find a moor, downland, wood, heath or footpath bordering farmland at dawn or dusk. That's the time you're most likely to hear the stags or bucks bellowing.

In more urban areas, deer parks, where deer are managed but roam freely within large, fenced enclosures, are usually good places to watch and listen at any time of day – from a safe distance.

Deer facts

- Males, females and their young are known by different names, depending on the species. Red deer and sika are stags, hinds and calves. Muntjac, fallow and Chinese water deer are bucks, does and fawns. While roe deer are bucks, does and kids.
- The 1923 novel, *Bambi, a Life in the Woods* by Austrian writer Felix Salten, followed the life of a male roe deer. It was originally written for an adult audience. However, it was so popular, it was made into picture books for children, a Walt Disney animation, Russian action films, a play and a ballet. It was also translated into over 30 languages.
- Even though roe deer mate between July and August, their fertilised eggs don't develop until January. They are the only deer species to delay implantation, a process known as embryonic diapause.
- Stags have different names depending on the number of points on their antlers. A monarch has 16, imperial 14 and a royal 12 points. A mature male deer without antlers is known as a hummel (from Old English *hamelian* meaning 'mutilate').
- Deer have no natural predators in the UK, except humans. Their main predator, the wolf, died out in the eighteenth century.

The cachers

Caching is just a fancy word for collecting, hoarding or hiding. Though cached files on your computer may leave you cold, there are fascinating examples of caching to be found in the natural world.

At this time of year, across the country, coal tits and nuthatches are hiding seeds in tree crevices and behind bark, a canny tactic for when cold weather makes food harder to find. Foxes will be concealing roadkill under bushes; wood mice will be hoarding autumn nuts. Even moles are burying worms in fortress mounds below ground. However, the cacher to beat all cachers is undoubtedly the jay.

Jays are mainly a woodland bird. If you live near to trees or woodland, there's a good chance you'll have seen the flash of their shimmering blue wing feathers, pinkish-buff chests and black moustaches, or have heard their rather unattractive screech. Yet, it's the jay's habit of collecting acorns that propels it into a caching league of its own.

In October and November, when oak leaves start to turn and acorns fall, jays begin to hide acorns. Not just a few beakfuls, but thousands upon thousands, with each jay potentially stuffing as many as 5,000 acorns into holes they have dug in the ground.

Competition is rife. Dominant jays will cache, move and steal from right under the beaks of lower ranking birds. Subordinates, on the other hand, are more furtive – stealing and hiding acorns away from the gaze of their superiors.

The maths is mind-boggling: with roughly 170,000 territories in the UK, that's 1.7 billion acorns cached each year – an astonishing feat for such a shy bird. And with acorn recovery rates as high as 75 per cent, it's clear that jays aren't just good at caching, they also have excellent memories.

Jay

Thankfully, that still leaves thousands of lost or forgotten acorns to sprout into new trees, and though it might seem the humble oak is a passive participant in this exchange, that's far from the truth. Over millennia, oaks have evolved successful tactics to promote the spread – and germination – of their seeds.

To start with, acorns make a hearty meal. They are nutritious and well worth the effort cachers spend collecting and hiding them. The oak counteracts this by giving acorns very little scent, making them devilishly hard to re-find. But the oak's master stroke is bombardment.

Every five to 10 years, all across the country, oaks go into seed production overdrive. Called a mast year, this bumper crop is more than even the most enthusiastic cacher could cope with. And though it may be costly in terms of the energy used by the tree to produce so many acorns, what better way to protect your genes?

In areas with fewer woods and where jays are less common, such as urban parks and open countryside, there's another cacher at work – the magpie. Magpies are also ardent acorn collectors and prefer less wooded landscapes. With tree planting a priority for the future of carbon capture, this established urban and farmland bird's fondness for acorn caching might just provide us with the help we need to plant more trees. This is good news for nature conservation, and good news for the climate.

If you're lucky enough to live near a mature oak tree, then a stakeout, when the acorns are just starting to fall, should provide a fascinating view of jays or magpies at work. A word of warning, though, they won't be impressed that you're watching. The trick is to be nonchalant. Don't stare. Pretend you haven't seen them. All corvids, including magpies and jays, are incredibly intelligent birds, so pretending to be as uninterested as possible, while still sneaking a few looks, will be your best tactic.

The forgotten visitors

They arrived unseen, and five months later, we hardly notice them leave. Yet each year an estimated 23 million redwings and fieldfares migrate to the UK from their summer breeding grounds as far away as Scandinavia and Russia. That's nearly six times more birds than the number of swallows, house martins, sand martins and swifts that travel to our shores to breed in spring.

If they were tiny, nondescript birds, it might be easier to understand their unremarked arrival. But with the redwing's distinctive rusty armpits, and the fieldfare's grey hood and bold black tail plumage, neither are particularly camouflaged nor small.

In truth, it's unfair to say no one sees them. Avid birdwatchers count and listen for them on vismig (visible migration) and nocmig (nocturnal migration) surveys and they are also visible to meteorologists who record them flying at high altitudes in vast flocks.

But for the rest of us, even those who live in more rural areas, they can go under the radar. One day the fields are empty, the next they're full of redwings and fieldfares, and we just accept and mostly ignore them.

Neither are they birds that have inspired many writers or poets to put pen to paper. There's a brief mention by Chaucer of the 'frosty fieldfare' in 1382 in *The Parliament of Fowls*, and John Clare alludes to 'fieldfares chatter in the whistling thorn' in his poem, 'Emmonsails Heath in Winter',

If it's a cold autumn with hard frosts, redwings and fieldfares will often appear in gardens, orchards and parks.

but compared to the nightingale or cuckoo, they don't play a leading role in English literature.

Folklore and myths around these understated birds are also hard to find. Kentish fishermen recalled stories of 'the herring spear'; a rushing sound heard on dark, still winter nights in the English Channel, which may or may not have been the wings of redwings whooshing overhead. In Suffolk, the early arrival of fieldfare was considered a sign of a hard winter. But surprisingly for birds that have been part of our autumn and winter landscape for hundreds of years, these stories aren't found countrywide.

So this year, make a point of going to see them. Their mass arrival usually peaks around mid-October. And as they often migrate at night, you might hear the eery 'tseep' of redwings passing overhead in the dark, even in the busiest of towns and cities. In more rural areas, new arrivals can often be spotted feeding in large flocks, like a river of birds, rippling and splashing across the fields, looking for worms and other invertebrates.

In late afternoon, before they roost in woodlands and copses, birds often feed in the hedgerows. Fieldfares can be particularly territorial and like to guard favourite food bushes, such as holly and hawthorn. They may even fly towards you, with a loud 'chack-chack' as a warning. They won't hurt you, but with their outstretched angel-wings they might make you jump, and your heart skip a beat.

If it's a cold autumn with hard frosts, redwings and fieldfares will often appear in gardens, orchards and parks, especially where there are windblown apples on the ground, or if food has been left out for them. If the cold weather continues, their numbers will often increase day by day, as food in the wild becomes harder to find.

Fieldfare

Perhaps our general apathy towards them is because we don't consider them 'ours', or don't think of this country as being their true home. Now is the time to seek them out. Get to know and admire these plucky visitors. If they arrived with the swallows in spring, would we notice and cherish them more?

Redwing

Fallen leaves

When did you last kick your way through a pile of leaves? As a child, you probably revelled in the activity every autumn, only too happy to don a hat and coat on a windy day. It's one of the simple pleasures of being young. Then time passes until finally you can't remember the last time you felt such carefree happiness.

In the grown-up world, attitudes to leaves can be a bit snooty. As an adult, you learn that fallen leaves should be blown, raked and vacuumed from your life. Decades of obsessing over neat and tidy green spaces have erased our leaf-kicking memories. But recently, attitudes towards leaves have started to change, and we're recognising how beneficial they are.

It's easy to see how we could take leaves for granted. They are everywhere. Yet from the very beginning, in spring, as they unfurl in all their chlorophyll beauty, they are locking up carbon dioxide and converting it into oxygen for us to breathe.

When summer arrives, leaves become food and shelter for wildlife, such as moths, beetles and birds. When temperatures cool in autumn, their colours rival any swatch from Farrow & Ball. Once they fall to the ground, hedgehogs, insects, frogs, toads and newts hide away beneath them, protected from the harsh winter elements.

We tend to notice the different colours of autumn leaves. This is all down to the weather and the unique mix of chemicals within their structure. If there have been a few frosty nights, chlorophyll in green leaves will have been destroyed, turning them yellow. If temperatures have been warmer, their water-soluble pigments can be stronger, even turning them a deep, vibrant red.

As leaves rot on the ground, they become the lifeblood of our soil, feeding the millions of soil microbes and fungi that have been a rich

source of cancer treatments and antibiotic drugs. Indeed, our first truly successful antibiotic, penicillin, came from a soil fungus. It's hoped that recent research into how microbes and fungi protect themselves from infections will lead to the development of new, more effective antibiotics.

As well as their medicinal value, leaves could also help us in the fight against climate change. Researchers in Canada have designed what they call an 'artificial' leaf. Instead of turning carbon dioxide and water into oxygen and sugars, this leaf turns it into oxygen and methanol. The hope is that this technology could enable the development of more climate-friendly fuels.

Go on, recapture those childhood feelings. Try kicking through a pile of fallen leaves and throwing them into the air. Cast off your inhibitions. Feel the leaves as they brush against your face, listen as they crinkle and crackle under your feet and breathe in their goodness. You could even invite a friend to join you.

If leaf-kicking really isn't your thing, then perhaps collecting them is. Gather up a handful and use them to create a design on the ground. Build out from the centre with circles of leaves, some big, some small, using different shapes, colours and textures. This ancient geometric design is known as a mandala, a Sanskrit word meaning 'circle'. Natural mandalas made from leaves can be a relaxing way to pass an hour, with the added benefit that it will bring a little bit of artistic beauty into the lives of anyone who's passing by.

House spiders

Have you noticed how every autumn, without fail, there are news stories about house-invading spiders together with directions for their removal? In a country of animal lovers, it's rare for a creature to be so universally despised and, more unusual still, for it to be linked to a phobia. This fear, as far as spiders go, seems deep-rooted and somewhat unfair. Why are so many of us so scared of them?

For around 11 months of the year, house spiders live with us as rarely seen, silent, rather useful tenants. It's not until the first few weeks in September that they break cover. This is mating season.

Some psychologists believe it could be an evolved response developed over thousands of years. Spiders can bite. This could make us ill and reduce our chances of survival, therefore it's best to run away. However, the UK doesn't have any deadly spiders, so even if you provoked one into giving you a nip, its bite would be no worse than a bee sting.

Other experts think the fear could be cultural, harking back to deadly epidemics during medieval times when spiders bore the brunt of people's anxieties. It's possible, but it seems if you ask people nowadays what they fear most about spiders, it's the erratic and speedy way they move, along with their long hairy legs, rather than their bite. Whatever the reasons for our irrational fears, it's a shame because the more we learn about spiders, the more we realise their scary reputation is wholly unwarranted.

The house spiders in our homes make up just a handful of the 650 species of arachnid living in the UK. Fast, dark brown and with eight long legs, house spiders may look creepy, but they eat many of the flies and other insects we'd rather not live with, so are superb pest controllers.

It's thought they moved inside our homes as long ago as Roman times, spinning their webs in quiet, undisturbed corners as they do today. They're not an aggressive or gregarious creature, and they've even adapted to life with central heating, hardly any water and not much food in our super-insulated modern dwellings. Some species rely on us so much they can't survive if moved outside.

For around 11 months of the year, house spiders live with us as rarely seen, silent, rather useful tenants. It's not until the first few weeks in September that they break cover. This is mating season. A time when fully grown male house spiders leave their webs in search of a mate. The spider you see scuttling across your living room floor or staring at you with its eight eyes from the bottom of the bath, isn't out to get you. It's more Romeo than assassin.

Female house spiders, on the other hand, don't roam far. They sit tight and wait to be discovered by an amorous male suitor. Once together, they'll mate several times and, for the next few weeks, the male will see off any interlopers. Eventually, with his mission accomplished and within the dusty confines of her cobweb, he'll die in her arms – or, more accurately, within her many legs.

If you're still finding spiders difficult to accept as housemates, maybe their medicinal webs will convince you. Research into house spider silk has found it to have antibacterial properties. Scientists at the University of Nottingham are developing an artificial spider silk with antibiotics attached. It's hoped this technology could be used in the production of wound dressings and surgical thread, which could even adjust to the number of bacteria present by releasing more antibiotics when needed. In the future, if you sustain a severe cut, the speed at which it heals might be down to these ground-breaking, house spider-inspired techniques.

With insect numbers in free fall, it's easy to see how the spider population could also suffer. So instead of – literally – throwing the book at them, we need to learn to love them more, or at least to respect them. That doesn't mean you have to become a fan of spiders overnight, but it could mean reading up about them, or taking a closer look when one appears.

If it's a house spider, see if it has boxing glove-shaped attachments on its palps (the two appendages in front of its legs). If it does, it's a male, and those gloves are its sexual organs; a handy way to carry sperm, and useful for waving around as it approaches a potential mate. If one scuttles across the hall, making you jump, remember that some house spiders can move half a metre (1½ft) per second; it might be an unsettling sight, but it is also pretty remarkable to be sharing your house with a record-breaking sprinter.

Autumn gales

'My soul is awakened, my spirit is soaring; And carried aloft on the winds of the breeze; For above and around me the wild wind is roaring.' Some 200 years after Anne, the youngest of the Brontë sisters, penned these words, a walk on a windy day can still make your spirits soar and awaken your soul. Freedom and release go hand in hand with the wind. As leaves swirl and dance, all you can do is watch, listen and breathe.

Are autumn gales a recognised annual event? Yes, and no. Some years might have more gales than others, and they can vary in their ferocity, but in most years we will usually experience them in some form or another. Their driving force, and the thing that influences the rest of our weather, is the jet stream.

The jet stream is a river of air in the northern hemisphere that flows from west to east some 10,000 metres (33,000ft) above the Earth's surface. It's largely controlled by differences in heat – cold polar air to the north and warmer air to the south – that cause changes to our wind speed and pressure.

In summer, when the difference between northern and southern temperatures is less pronounced, the jet stream usually lies to the north of the UK and we experience more settled, drier weather. However, during the winter, when temperature variations are more extreme, the jet stream intensifies, dragging weather systems directly over the country from the east.

It's these easterly winds that cause our autumn gales. Sometimes, if the jet stream stays lodged in the same position, these

There are few things that top the excitement of being out in an autumn gale.

systems become trapped and turn into more prolonged and severe storms.

As our planet continues to warm due to climate change, extreme weather events such as these are likely to increase. Scientists predict an increase from our current seven days a year of prolonged and severe rain, to nine or even 11 days. Not only will this bring more flooding, power cuts and disruption to our lives, but also devastation to our wildlife. Veteran and ancient trees will fall, and hundreds of seal pups on exposed beaches will die. Weather can be cruel, but just how bad it's likely to get will depend on how quickly and effectively the world can act to slow down and perhaps reverse the effects of global warming.

When a gale approaches, there is always the temptation to batten down the hatches, draw the curtains and snuggle up on the sofa. But perhaps we all need to throw a little caution to the wind and blow some cobwebs away.

There are few things that top the excitement of being out in an autumn gale. It's a primitive, wild and individual experience. Though we normally shun it, this type of weather can reconnect us with nature. How the wind feels against your skin, the sound or the taste can, as Brontë said, reawaken your soul.

Perhaps this is not advisable in winds of force 8 or above (that's definitely the time to stay indoors and watch a good film) but take a chance on a lower-grade autumn gale. The sort that's windy, but not throw-you-to-the-ground fierce. It doesn't matter where you go – although away from trees is probably safer – as anywhere can be wild in wild weather.

The horse chestnut tree

There's a theory that you can tell someone's age by the way they walk past a horse chestnut tree. If they stop, compelled to scan the ground and start scrabbling under leaves, you know they are generation conker.

For many, finding a horse chestnut tree rekindles childhood memories. The agonising wait for the tree's spiked seed casings to turn from green to brown. A wind strong enough to make them fall, scattering burnished brown conkers in every direction. Trepidation as you picked them up, checking they were still whole. The crushing disappointment when they weren't; the euphoria when they were.

In the autumn, when we were young, life revolved around playing conkers. A skewer was used (very carefully) to make a hole through the conker. This was threaded with a length of string or an old shoelace and tied in a sturdy knot. Then the games could begin! You took it in turns with your opponent to hit each other's dangling conker until one was smashed to the ground. In England, a winning conker was dubbed a one-er, then a two-er, and so on, after each successful bout. In Scotland they were called a bully-one and a bully-two. In some variations of the game, the winning conker took on the score of the beaten player. Often, ingenious methods were employed to harden conkers. You might boil them in vinegar, dry them in the oven, or keep them for an entire year to harden. Whether any of these techniques worked is debatable – but we still did them.

Although the horse chestnut tree wasn't introduced to the UK from the Balkans until the end of the sixteenth century, it's known that a form of 'conkers' was probably being played before that, with empty snail shells or hazelnuts. However, proper conker playing wasn't recorded until 1843,

and it's still being played today. The World Conker Championships in Northamptonshire has taken place since 1965, and still attracts competitors from around the world. But what about younger players? A few years ago, when a rumour circulated that conker playing was going to be banned in school playgrounds due to health and safety concerns, there was a national uproar. Happily, it wasn't true. However, it took the government's Health and Safety Executive to issue a statement debunking the myth before the furore died down.

For a relative newcomer to the UK, the horse chestnut has still attracted a surprising number of local customs and old wives' tales since its arrival. If you carry three conkers in your pocket, it's supposed to ensure you always have money – or aids virility (take your pick). The longer the spines on a conker's casing, the longer and more severe the winter will be. If you're an arachnophobe, placing conkers in the corner of a room is supposed to act as a spider deterrent – though there's no scientific proof this works.

The trees, with their widely spreading boughs, are renowned as magnificent shade-giving trees, and were often planted outside a blacksmith's forge to shade waiting customers. They line the streets of some of the most fashionable European cities, such as the Avenue des Champs-Élysées in Paris.

The name horse chestnut is thought to have arisen from conkers once being administered as a cough medicine and coat enhancer for horses. Even though they're mildly poisonous to humans, conkers were ground into flour by the Victorians. Aescin, a compound with anti-inflammatory properties, was extracted from conkers and used to treat sprains, varicose veins and even piles.

Conkers also contain saponins, a soap-like chemical, which can be made into a DIY, eco-friendly alternative to laundry detergent, but probably one of the most unusual uses for conkers was during the First World War. Running low on cordite supplies (a propellant used in the production of explosives), research chemist Chaim Weizmann (who later became president of Israel) was tasked by the British Government with finding a new way of producing acetone, a key ingredient in cordite production. When conkers were found to contain acetone, a public campaign paid children to collect them in their thousands. A secret cordite factory was built in Dorset, but sadly, many of the conkers went to waste as they were found to be hard to process.

This year, whatever your age, make a point of finding a horse chestnut tree. They don't tend to be found in woods, so look in parks, commons and on roadsides. Kick through their brown, crispy, hand-shaped leaves, break open the spiky outer shell of the seed, and fill your pockets with smooth, mahogany conkers. Can there be a pastime that's more enjoyable in autumn?

Sweet or horse chestnut?

The sweet and horse chestnut aren't related, but their seeds are similar. Sweet chestnut trees were first introduced during Roman times, with some truly ancient specimens still growing in the UK. Their edible nuts are found inside prickly casings and they can not only be made into a gluten-free alternative to wheat flour but are also used in stuffings, or roasted and eaten whole, especially at Christmas. Unlike the hand-shaped leaves of the horse chestnut, the leaves of the sweet chestnut are long and serrated, and its bark spirals like a gnarled staircase up and around the tree.

Sweet chestnut

Fungi

Fungi are a bit of an oddity. They're neither animal nor plant, they look decidedly strange, have a kingdom all of their own and are everywhere. Over 15,000 species of fungi have been identified in the UK, and 148,000 throughout the world. Although this sounds like a lot, it's probably just 5 per cent of the species likely to exist.

Fungi are beneath our feet in the soil, in rivers and seas, and live inside and on animals and plants. They even thrive in and on humans. Yet our understanding of different fungi, how they live, what they do and how they do it, is limited. We're only now recognising the value of conserving them.

Trying to define fungi is difficult because they're so varied, but one feature they share is the way they obtain nutrients. Fungi don't eat food and digest it in their bodies like animals. Nor do they photosynthesise like most plants. Instead, they grow around or into their food, releasing enzymes that digest it externally before absorbing the nutrients.

Most of us, when we hear the word fungi, probably think of the mould on our week-old bread, or the spore-bearing fruiting bodies that pop up in woodlands and meadows as poisonous toadstools or edible mushrooms. The largest living organism on Earth, which covers some 965ha (almost 2,400 acres), is a fungus. Discovered in 1998 in the Blue Mountains of Oregon, USA, *Armillaria ostoyae* has been spreading underground, using a root-like web of mycelium and thread-like hyphae for some 2,000 years.

It's not alone. Most fungi species live out of sight below ground, only coming to the surface when they need to reproduce and spread their spores. The vital role they play as decomposers, parasites and partners to plants is nevertheless vital to the health of our natural world.

Fly agaric

The job of decomposition falls to the saprotrophic fungi, such as the oyster mushroom. Along with bacteria and other microbes, these fungi help to break down dead organic matter by either absorbing the nutrients themselves or releasing them back into the soil to help other living things. If they didn't exist, the natural cycles of decomposition would collapse, and more carbon and nitrogen would be released into the atmosphere.

Parasitic fungi are less altruistic. The spores of some species take advantage of lesions or tears on plants and, by invading this vulnerable tissue, cause weaknesses, disease and sometimes even the death of their host – as is the case with ash dieback. Other parasitic fungi make use of insects, such as beetles, to help them spread within their chosen host. This happens in Dutch elm disease, caused by a fungus called *Ophiostoma novo-ulmi*, and so far is thought to have killed over 25 million elms in the UK. Even humans are not immune: conditions such as athlete's foot and ringworm are both caused by parasitic fungi.

The largest living organism on Earth, which covers some 965ha (almost 2,400 acres), is a fungus.

With traits similar to saprotrophic and parasitic fungi, mycorrhizal fungi develop an altogether more symbiotic and mutually beneficial relationship with their plant partners. Mycorrhizal fungi generate vast networks carrying water, carbon, nitrogen, phosphorus and carbohydrates between plants and other fungi. Think of it as an interconnected web of threads, taking resources from plants that have more and transporting them to those that have less, like the Robin Hood of the plant world. They can even transmit warnings of insect attacks between plants.

Mycorrhizal fungi are an integral part of a vast beneficial network –

90 per cent of our land-based plants are thought to rely on them to thrive. This understanding has literally changed the way scientists look at our environment: a woodland is no longer a random collection of individual trees. It's a community looking out for each other – helped by fungi.

Next time you notice a bright red fungi or ring of mushrooms in autumn, pay it a little more attention. Beneath your feet is a whole other world keeping our environment healthy and safe. Some people think fungi could save the world. Maybe, just maybe, they will.

Oyster mushroom

First frost

The first frost of the year can catch you unawares. One minute you're basking in the warmth of an Indian summer; the next, Jack Frost is coating autumn seed-heads with ice. As you throw T-shirts into storage and scrabble for a woolly jumper, remember that it's good that the weather is changing. We need it to change. Especially from one season to the next – it's what keeps our natural environment in balance.

Though it's tempting to creep back to bed with a cup of tea on those first chilly mornings, there's something else you could consider. The Danes call it *hygge*: a word to describe the comfort and warmth derived from doing simple, cosy things. And what could be simpler than a walk (wrapped up warm of course) to appreciate the first frost?

You'll need to be quick as those first few frosts rarely last long. Try to get out into your favourite green space and listen to the crunch of newly formed ice underfoot. Breathe in the clean, crisp scent of frozen earth and feel the tingle of ice crystals on your skin as you brush past a hanging branch. As the sun rises and turns the silvered landscape pink, watch your breath unfurl into wisps, like spiralling smoke.

Frost can be magical to experience, but there's no genuine mystery to its science. On a cold, clear, wind-free night, freezing temperatures turn water vapour in our atmosphere into ice, which in the UK is likely to cause a ground or grass frost.

Ground frost forms on trees, plants and even man-made surfaces when the surface temperature drops below freezing. When roads and concrete are frost-free, but the grass has cooled enough to freeze, it's known as grass frost. Though not an official meteorological term, weather forecasters tend to use it as a warning for gardeners to protect their tender plants.

But frost doesn't herald the end of all plants in the veg patch. For some it's a blessing. After a frost, root crops – such as carrots, beetroot and swedes – produce their own sugary anti-freeze, which can mean sweeter vegetables. A bonus for Sunday lunch.

When will this year's first frost arrive? That's hard to say. Our seasons are shifting and merging. Spring is becoming warmer, summer is less predictable with heatwaves and washouts, and seems to merge into autumn. And winter? Though we associate winter with frost, and the meteorological calendar says winter starts on 1 December, records show some areas of the UK will not have experienced a first frost until well after that date. And other areas, especially in Cornwall, won't experience a frost at all. It makes you wonder how long it will be before frost becomes a thing of the past for much of the country.

As we struggle to keep our world cool, let's celebrate every frost we still get, especially the first ones of the year.

As we struggle to keep our world cool, let's celebrate every frost we get, especially the first ones of the year. Cosy socks, gloves and a hat are a must if you want to experience that 'hygge' feeling. Consider taking a camera, phone or sketch pad and pencils to record what you see. Or, if you prefer, write notes. Take a hot drink and a snack. If you're in the garden, this could be your morning cuppa. For a park excursion, perhaps take a flask of warming soup. Food and drink consumed outside always tastes better. Try to get close to the ice. Look at a frozen leaf or ice-covered blade of grass. Stamp the moment into your memory and then stamp your feet. When the cold creeps into your bones it's time to hurry home.

Winter roosts

Around the feet of weary shoppers two pied wagtails skip across the concrete paving stones in search of tiny insects. Their tails bob in time with the footsteps, part of the urban landscape. These birds go unnoticed, even though they are present year-round.

Above them, high on the flat roofs of nearby shops, more wagtails are gathering. Their high-pitched 'chizick' bounces off the concrete walls, but is drowned out by the growl of passing cars. Birds continue to arrive. Some launch into the air as if propelled by their bobbing tails, then drop into the surrounding trees.

Others follow. Slowly at first, in dribs and drabs, then in larger groups as they squeeze onto the branches of the trees to roost. There's bickering and pecking between neighbours as they settle. If the shoppers were to look up, they'd see this winter spectacle. But no one does, they are in too much of a hurry to get home.

This scene is not unusual. Pied wagtails often find safety in numbers in busy and bright areas of our towns, even though, or maybe because, we don't notice them. With over 470,000 UK pairs breeding each summer, you're never far away from a pied wagtail.

Though their natural winter roosts are reed beds, nowadays factory roofs, shopping centres and even hospital courtyards can provide them with shelter, warmth and protection from hungry predators. Gathering in such large groups each night can also be useful for sharing information about feeding sites and checking out mates. Jackdaws and rooks do the same, often using the same copses and woods in which their kin have gathered for hundreds of years.

Many bird species roost, especially in the winter. Even tiny wrens, the UK's most common bird, roosts for warmth and shelter. Weighing just

10g (⅓oz), wrens are in danger of losing much of their body weight from trying to keep warm, so finding roosts of nine or ten wrens huddled together is not unusual. In Norfolk in 1969, 61 wrens were found crammed into a single nest box.

Whether it's wagtails in a shopping centre, starlings on the metalwork of a pier or house sparrows in a roof space, winter is the perfect time to look for winter roosts. Experiencing the excited jabbering of roosting birds has got to be one of nature's hidden-in-plain-sight gems. Not only is seeing a roost bound to make you smile, there's also something awe-inspiring about the mass gathering of any species of wildlife.

So, whether you hope to see a murmuration of thousands of starlings dancing across the sky, or a more modest house sparrow roost in an overgrown privet hedge in the centre of town, finding out where roosts are taking place is all down to insider knowledge.

In Norfolk in 1969, 61 wrens were found crammed into a single nest box.

Search online. Check out local online bird forums. Ask questions. The birding community are a friendly bunch, and love to help people see and appreciate wildlife. Talk to people in your community who have lived in the area for a long time. They'll often know where the local jackdaw roost is, where the greenfinches gather at night, or where the wagtails roost in the trees. And the next time you are walking home on a cold winter's evening, don't forget to look up.

Pied wagtails

Long shadows

Have you noticed how places look and feel different in winter? Not just the obvious differences, such as bare tree branches or muddy footpaths. The landscape looks as if it's been put through a mangle and stretched out of all proportion. We know it's just a dance between the angle of the sun, light and shade, but this illusion can still bring a special something to a winter's day.

Shadows have always preyed on our most primitive fears. Folklore warns of causing suffering if you tread on a person's shadow. In the biblical underworld, the dead lived in perpetual shadow. In horror movies, villains and monsters always lurk in and jump out of the shadows.

You could say though that shadows have received a bad rap; the poet Sylvia Plath called them 'the most beautiful thing in the world'. As well as being mysterious, there's intense beauty in the long shadows of winter. Trees become earthbound. Their branches are linocut shadows ripe for climbing; their trunks a grassy toboggan to ride down a hill.

Back lit by the low sun, even your own shadow takes on a different persona. Legs become stilts and arms grow ridiculously long; your body becomes the elongated shape you'd see in a distorted mirror at a fairground sideshow. Of course, our out-of-proportion shadows are just the result of the Earth's tilt away from the sun, something we can also use to our advantage.

Over the centuries, we've found many uses for shadows. Ancient mathematicians used shadows for measuring the height of the Great Pyramids and they were even used to calculate the circumference of the Earth. But probably the most widely recognised use has been telling the time. Still sold today, the sundial, with its round, flat dial and thin, upright rod – or gnomon – used to cast a shadow, is a simple but elegant way of tracking the passing of the hours.

Steep, north-facing hills, or even the ramparts of hill forts or castles, are great places to spot long shadows on a bright winter's day. Stand at the top of the hill and, depending on how low the sun is, your own shadow could reach to the bottom. Wave your arms, shake your legs and have a bit of fun. No one will care, but if you feel shy take a young family member with you. Children know how much fun it is to play games with shadows. We've just forgotten.

Though we associate shadows with the sun, it's not the only celestial body to make them. Moon shadows, cast on the clearest, brightest nights of the year, are also some of the most magical. Take a friend on an evening walk – experiencing something as special as moon shadows is more enjoyable when you have company. Make sure you leave the house when it's still light, so your eyes have time to adjust. Try not to use a torch and choose a place you know well. Although it won't look the same at night as during the day, its general familiarity should be reassuring. Now relax. Look around you and take in the beauty of the shadows of the glistening silver moon.

We know the sun rises in the east and sets in the west and, in the Northern Hemisphere, shadows move from west to east. So, if you're out walking during the day and get lost, and need to know where north is to get back on track, here's what to do:

Finding north

Find a flat spot and a branch 1m (3ft) long. Push the branch into the ground so that it casts a shadow. Mark the tip of the shadow with an object, such as a stone – this is west. Wait 15 minutes and mark the new position of the shadow's tip – this will point east. Now stand with the first mark on your left and the second on your right and you'll be facing due north.

Tawny owls

You wake to a strange sound, almost as if someone is making ghost noises outside your bedroom window. 'Wooooooooooo-wooooooooo!' Halloween is over, and it's highly unlikely your friends would bother with a spooky prank at 3am, so you peer out between the curtains. The view is lit by a silvery moon. You wait, and just when you're about to get back into bed, there's a movement in a nearby tree and you see something silhouetted against the moon. An owl. A tawny.

You hear the trembling 'woooooooo' again. A pulsing, quivering noise, followed by a sharp 'ker-wik'. There's a pair, and they're close together, perhaps examining a hole in the tree's rotten trunk. In the cold air of a winter night, you can feel the vibration of their calls running up your fingers and into your chest. It's primal. A wild noise that drags you into an unknown, monotone world.

Autumn and winter are when tawny owls are at their noisiest. It's thought both males and females make the quivering sound when inspecting prospective nesting sites. A tree with a hollow trunk is likely to tick all their house hunting boxes. Good access, right size, excellent location and with a plentiful supply of wood mice and voles nearby.

But if you were to ask most people what sound an owl makes – especially a tawny owl – they're likely to reply with the one we all learned when we were young: 'tu-whit, tu-whoo'. And though this onomatopoeia isn't wrong, this sound is made by two owls calling to one another, not a single bird. The female tawny makes the 'tu-whit' (or, more accurately, a sharp 'ker-wick') and her mate replies with a languorous 'who-hoooo'.

The 3am callers will have a territory covering several hectares, which includes your garden and many others. And though there are an estimated 50,000 breeding pairs of tawnies in the UK, they lead a life that is so secretive you may never have known they lived so close.

Research has shown that each owl's call is distinct, either by length, structure or pitch. So, not only will they recognise each other's calls, but also those of their neighbours outside their own territory. And woe betide any unfamiliar owl that strays too close. For young, territory-less owls, early winter can be a dangerous time. Chased from their natal home by their parents, they often stray into unknown territories. Then it won't be a soft 'woooooooo' you'll hear, but blood-curdling shrieks as these young interlopers are pursued and unceremoniously evicted for their trespassing.

If you live within the territory of a pair of tawny owls, you're in luck. Though you might not hear the quiver of their house-hunting call, the 'ker-wick' and 'who-hoooo' is already a call you probably recognise.

On nights of great activity, when youngsters fly through fiercely guarded territories, and resident owls can be on high alarm, that's the time to go outside. For most of the year, tawny owls lead relatively quiet lives, so when you hear them calling there is definitely something important going on.

If you do, it's worth jumping out of bed, wrapping up warm and venturing out into the dark. Even if you only do it once. It doesn't matter if you live in the centre of town or in the countryside, there's little to compare to the sound of an owl, or two owls, calling in the darkness, but you can't appreciate the experience fully without being outside. Their calls will move as they fly from tree to tree or roof to roof, you may even see them, flying low, doing the rounds of their territory, hunting for food. You'll feel as if it's just you and the owls. Then, once you go back inside, the hardest thing will be getting back to sleep!

Seed heads

With brilliant feathers of gold, red and black, and a liquid, twittering song, a flock of goldfinches flows over the frozen fields in search of food. Dead stems bounce under their grasp. Seed heads explode into monochrome fireworks and sharp, investigative beaks tease apart knapweed cones and teasels, or the beards of wild clematis and thistle. Then they're off. A river of darting eyes, wings and chattering calls, skimming the frozen earth.

Although it's hard to deny the beauty of an ice-shackled landscape, for our wild birds, this weather makes it hard to survive. Seed eaters, such as the goldfinch, greenfinch and chaffinch, rely on a constant supply of seeds – most of which have all but disappeared from our countryside. Changes in farming methods, and a drive for cheaper, mass-market food, have removed many of the plants they relied on, leaving field margins bare of the 'weeds' they need, as well as fewer hedgerows.

The pincushion flowers of teasel, that were purple-petalled and nectar-rich in summer, are now pounced on by hungry, seed-eating birds. With their specially adapted beaks, goldfinches have no problem prising the protein rich seeds out of the prickly flowerheads.

There was a time when we revered this prickliness ourselves. The heads of a relative of our native wild teasels were used to tease the fibres and raise the nap in woollen cloth, first by hand and then incorporated into a machine called a gig mill. Later, as machines were modernised, the natural teasels were replaced by human-made alternatives, although some weavers still swear by fuller's teasels, claiming they are kinder to the cloth.

With its habit of frothing over hedgerows, the feather-like seed heads of another important seed producer, wild clematis, have long been appreciated for their winter beauty. They have no doubt brightened the

day of many a weary traveller – coining them another of its common names, 'traveller's joy'. This fast-growing native plant is the less showy cousin of the cultivated clematis we nurture in our gardens, and in autumn and winter its white, feathery styles are carried away on the breeze to ensure the seeds' dispersal. It is another valuable source of wild food, and birds pounce on the seeds before they float away. As the new year approaches, charms of goldfinches descend on hedgerows fuzzed with 'old man's beard', another of the plant's common names, and it can be fun to watch them as they give it a trim.

Our association with this plant goes back a long way. Its woody, flexible stems were used for centuries to weave into rustic baskets, a traditional skill that is being rediscovered. Swiss scientists have found that it was used to make rope as far back as the Stone Age.

Nowadays, you don't need to travel far to appreciate the beauty and usefulness of winter seed heads, as you can grow your own. Wild plants like teasel, devil's-bit scabious and black knapweed will all blend effortlessly into formal planting designs in garden flowerbeds. While pollinator-friendly cultivars, such as echinacea, sedums, alliums and rudbeckias, will also give an interesting structure to a winter garden.

Try not to go overboard with garden tidying in the autumn. Leave as many stems and flowerheads as possible; prop them up if they are looking a bit floppy. You'll not only see birds such as greenfinches, goldfinches and chaffinches feeding on the seeds, but their dried foliage makes a perfect hiding place for overwintering insects, such as ladybirds, who need a place to tuck themselves away. And when – or if – it snows or there's a hard frost, you'll have your very own winter wonderland of gleaming, crystallised seed heads.

Snow

I wonder if the snow loves the trees and fields,
that it kisses them so gently? And then it covers them up
snug, you know, with a white quilt;
and perhaps it says, Go to sleep, darlings,
till the summer comes again.

FROM *THROUGH THE LOOKING-GLASS* (1871) BY LEWIS CARROLL

The weather's been cold. Colder than usual. One morning, you wake up and instinctively know something is different, but you can't quite figure out what. As you lie in bed listening, the sounds outside seem muffled and distant. Your room feels brighter, even though the curtains are closed. You worry you may have overslept. Then you peep through the curtains, and everything makes sense: snow.

Snow has become a rarity for most of us. Obviously, the further north and higher up you live, the more likely you are to see it – Scotland still has an average of 38 days of falling snow or sleet a year. Cornwall, on the other hand, may see just eight days of snow at most. And if you factor in the warming effects of climate change, waking up to an unexpected blanket of snow is going to become increasingly rare.

To be fair to the meteorologists, snow is tricky to predict. Even when there is cold air from the north or east that could bring snow, the sea that surrounds us warms it just enough to produce rain, or maybe slushy sleet.

A prolonged period of high pressure, or clear skies and plummeting temperatures mixed with either a rain-bearing weather front or cold air passing over the sea from the north or east, can both cause snow. But both are becoming less common.

Today, it's hard to imagine a prolonged period of snow, but 60 years ago, snow began to fall all over the UK just before Christmas Day and carried on until March. Snowdrifts lay 6m (20ft) deep. Even the sea froze around the shore in some places. The winter of 1963 was the UK's coldest since 1740, with temperatures consistently reaching -20°C (-4°F) degrees. Currently, the UK experiences around 50 days a year below 0°C (32°F), but with temperatures rising, that figure is expected to fall. Some areas in the south of England are already experiencing frost-free, let alone snow-free, winters.

Nowadays, snow is often newsworthy, and should certainly be celebrated for its uniqueness. Each flake that falls has six sides, or points, and no two flakes are ever the same. Some of those formed in warmer but dryer temperatures become flat, hexagonal plates with a star-shaped

centre. Others that crystallise at very low temperatures with plenty of moisture grow into intricate branched, tree-like shapes called dendrite snowflakes.

Some areas in the south of England are already experiencing frost-free, let alone snow-free, winters.

There's definitely something magical about a fresh fall of snow, and when it happens at night, it's a great excuse for some early-morning nature sleuthing. Most of us are unfamiliar with the visitors to our gardens in the hours of darkness, but a snowfall leaves us tantalising clues. Though it's tempting to stay indoors during cold weather, pulling on as many jumpers, coats and woolly socks as possible and getting outside to look for animal prints is well worth the effort.

Prints that are dog-like, slim and long-clawed are most likely a fox. Badger prints are also long with five toe pads side by side. Deer leave two long-pronged hoof marks with a gap in between, as well as telltale black, berry-like droppings. Then there are the bird prints: the confused, erratic lines and circles left by wood pigeons and blackbirds searching for food at dawn. Follow the prints. Imagine the creatures that made them, the harsh world they inhabit and the difficulties they overcome at this time of year. Then maybe cut up some apples and put them out in the garden to help them.

Meteors

To see shooting stars, it must be a dark winter's night, one with little or no moon and a sky that's clear of clouds. Leave the glow of town behind and pick your way across your chosen open space. Then sit down and look up: it's time to watch stars flash across the sky and make a wish.

December is a great time to spot shooting stars or, to give them their proper name, meteor showers (from the Greek *meteōros*, meaning 'high in the sky'). In fact, these slingshots of light aren't stars at all. They're streams of light from cosmic dust, sometimes as small as grains of sand, that blaze sparkler-like as they enter the earth's atmosphere.

Meteor showers are a well-known and regular phenomenon. From the bright, fast Lyrids in April to Perseid's light show in August, you could watch them every month of the year. Geminids meteors burst into our atmosphere in the first half of December at speeds of up to 34km (21 miles) per second, and of all the showers, they are considered the best.

Spectacular to watch, they are also somewhat unusual. First recorded in the 1860s, unlike most meteor showers the Geminids don't arise from comet debris, but instead come from a stream of dust left behind by a rare blue asteroid called 3200 Phaethon. From white to yellow – with a smattering of green, blue and red – it's thought this celestial firework display is intensifying every year.

If you'd like to see it, you'll need to plan. First, check the weather forecast. A clear, cloudless and still night is best (and most comfortable) for meteor spotting. As the Geminid meteor shower peaks around the middle of the month, check the moon phase. A new moon will mean the sky will be darker, making it easier to see any shooting stars. The International Dark-Sky Association has identified areas across the country that are 'naturally dark at night and free of light pollution', so it's

Perseid meteor shower

These slingshots of light aren't stars at all. They're streams of light from cosmic dust, sometimes as small as grains of sand, that blaze sparkler-like as they enter the earth's atmosphere.

worth finding out if there is one of these dark sky reserves nearby – the UK has some of the largest in Europe.

Try to find a wide, open, safe space away from the light pollution from nearby towns and cities. If you'd rather not be alone, invite a friend. Wrap up warm. Take a chair, blanket and flask, as well as plenty of snacks, as you could be meteor-gazing for some time.

There's no need to take a telescope or binoculars. Allow your eyes at least 35 to 40 minutes to adjust to the dark once you arrive at your stargazing destination – the perfect opportunity to get comfortable and sip a hot chocolate.

Each meteor shower has a 'radiant', a point in the sky from where it seems to emanate. The Geminids' radiant is near to the star Castor in the Gemini constellation. In the northern hemisphere, Castor can be located by looking towards the south-western sky, finding Orion's Belt, and looking above and to the left.

Or, if you prefer, use an app on your phone or a printout from the internet to direct you. Then relax, let your eyes linger on a dark area of sky near – but not on – the Geminid radiant. Meteors are quick, so you'll miss them if you look too intently at the point where they begin. Then all that's left to do is sit back and enjoy this natural phenomenon – when you see your first shooting star, don't forget to make a wish.

Robins

It's often the first bird to sing before dawn, and the last to be heard at night. But what is it that makes the robin so keen to warble from dawn to dusk in the depths of winter?

There's no denying that here in the UK we have a thing for robins. They're our poster bird for festive cards and decorations. Friendly, trusting even, as they hop around our feet in the garden. There's invariably a robin singing, apparently just for us, from a branch nearby. They take top spot in 'favourite bird' surveys, and many people swear by the saying: 'When robins appear, loved ones are near.' Yet, our cheeky garden companions aren't all they seem.

It's a sad fact, but robins aren't as obsessed with us as we are with them. They are, however, obsessed with territory – and that territory probably includes our patch. When a robin sings, it's just as likely to be saying keep off my land as serenading you, but don't take this rebuff to heart. It isn't aiming its aggression at you, but woe betide any rival robin that ventures onto its turf. It is understandable. If they are to survive the freezing night temperatures of winter, territory – and that means land with plenty of food and shelter – becomes a matter of life or death.

In winter, both males and females defend their own patch. They divide their time between singing, seeing off intruders and building fat reserves to see them through the night. No wonder their song can sound a little mournful on frosty December mornings.

However, when the breeding season arrives – sometimes as early

They are, however, obsessed with territory, and that territory probably includes our patch.

as January, if it's mild – the males and females pair up; this is when the song dial is turned up and territorial disputes with competitors can explode.

Fights start, as most fights do, with posturing and a slanging match. A male robin might be seen dancing from branch to branch, showing off his flaming red breast to his foe, while flinging melodic insults. Unfortunately, if neither bird backs down, the situation can take a darker turn. Bloody fights are not unheard of, sometimes leading to injury and even death.

Why then, when we encounter robins (and with over six million breeding territories in the UK, it's highly likely), do they seem so friendly? For the rest of Europe, it's a different story. Many robins are shy, even retiring, and skulk in thick woodland. Who can blame them? Centuries of being hunted and trapped in the southern Mediterranean can take its toll. Thankfully, in the UK we don't have the same history when it comes to robins. To them, we mimic the wild boar of old, rummaging through the rich soil with our garden spades, digging up invertebrates, a veritable smorgasbord of tasty treats for a hungry bird.

There aren't many places you won't find a robin. From your garden, local park, green space or even while walking down an urban side street, you're likely to hear its warbling song. High to begin with, the notes descend to a lower pitch but increase in tempo. Some phrases are quick, others slow; they can be long or short and punctuated by pauses. The song is so exquisite it has even been mistaken for a nightingale.

Hazel catkins

After the indulgences of the festive period, it's sometimes hard to make it through the early months of the year with their dark mornings, long nights and chilly temperatures. Trees and shrubs look lifeless and bare and spring still seems far away. But look more closely, and a slow reawakening is already taking place. From January, hazel catkins are lengthening and shimmering in the breeze like forgotten Christmas decorations.

The word catkin comes from the Middle Dutch, *katteken*, meaning 'kitten', possibly a nod to their resemblance to cat's tails and the soft furriness of some varieties. Hazel catkins are definitely in the cat's-tail camp and never assume the silky fluffiness of other catkins, such as pussy willow. Instead, if you run your fingers down the 240 or so individual flowers in one hazel catkin, it feels more like a string of tiny beads.

As each catkin matures, swells and opens, it releases a pepper pot of pollen for the wind to pollinate nearby female flowers. Though a large display of male hazel catkins is impressive, the female flowers are extremely hard to find. Hazels are monoecious, meaning they have both male and female blooms present on the same plant, but the female flowers are minuscule. Look for swollen, bud-like bumps on the same stems as the male catkins, and the tiny blood-red styles of the female flowers will eventually reveal themselves. It's hard to imagine something so small and delicate could ever grow into a hard-shelled hazelnut.

Humans have made use of the hazel for thousands of years. A fragment of a burned hazel shell dating back 10,000 years was discovered in 2019 on an archaeological dig in Scotland. The nuts were easy to store and transport and could be ground into a bread flour. By the time of the Domesday Book in 1086, hazel was being extensively coppiced (cut to the

ground to stimulate fresh growth) across the English lowlands. We relied heavily on hazel. It was used for everything, from hurdle (fence) making and walking sticks to house building as the wattle in wattle and daub. Its flexible stems were formed into small, lightweight coracle boats for river fishing, used as stakes for thatching or woven into baskets. Plus, until the 1800s, when coke and coal took over, it was a major source of fuel. As recently as the early twentieth century, Holy Cross Day on 14 September was a school holiday for children to harvest hazelnuts. This was often followed in November by the excitement of Nutcrack Night when the nuts would be opened.

As one of our most ancient native plants, hazel also features heavily in folklore. Not only would eating the nuts grant inspiration and wisdom, but a hazel staff also provided protection and was coveted by shepherds and pilgrims. To find water, you could use its forked branches for divining, or if you required a fairy, one of the best places to look was underneath a hazel tree.

Nowadays, old coppicing techniques are being practised again and are used by conservation organisations to encourage wildlife species, such as bluebells, nightingales and fritillary butterflies, back into our woodlands. Its foliage may even help to slow climate change. Research has shown that feeding hazel leaves to cows reduces the amount of methane and nitrogen they expel without affecting their milk yield.

It's easy to appreciate the beauty of a hazel in winter. With so many other trees still dormant, a hedgerow of hazel lit by winter sunshine, with its golden catkins cascading from its branches, is a captivating sight.

Common frogs

But best of all was the warm thick slobber
Of frogspawn that grew like clotted water.

<small>FROM 'DEATH OF A NATURALIST' (1966) BY SEAMUS HEANEY</small>

After enduring thick jumpers for what feels like months, a warmer day will eventually dawn. Though it's likely to be accompanied by grey skies, drizzle and murk, and may not feel like a cause for celebration, this shift in temperature brings change. Bulbs send up vivid green shoots. Birds become more vocal. And, though it's not quite spring, you can tell that nature's on the move.

Around this time, listen out for something unusual. Late at night, as you're rushing to put out the bins, you might notice an odd mechanical noise. At first the sound resembles a chapter of tiny motorbikes trundling up the road, but as you walk towards it, gear changes will morph into the mating croaks of male common frogs.

For most of the year, frogs slip under our radar, but that doesn't mean they are not there. If you're lucky enough to live within a few hundred metres of a pond, big or small, you won't be far from a frog. As they overwinter in abandoned animal burrows, under leaves or buried in compost heaps, it's tempting to think they would stay hidden year-round if it wasn't for their need to reproduce.

As the temperatures start to rise, male common frogs emerge first and march determinedly towards the nearest fresh water. Those that have overwintered at the bottom of ponds don't have far to go. Once they converge at the water's edge, they pump up their throats and sing.

It doesn't take female frogs long to respond. Within a day, watercourses will be full of frog love songs and shining eyes. Armed with

special sticky pads on their feet, males make sure they stick close to receptive females, so they can be in just the right place when she spawns. With so many frogs converging to mate, it's just as well they can breathe through their skin and nostrils – in the scuffle of mating, many get pushed underwater.

Within hours, Heaney's 'warm thick slobber' of spawn will appear in the shallows. A short while later, the frogs will melt back into the undergrowth, their work complete. If the spawn isn't eaten by birds, fish or newts, it will develop into wriggling, water-bound tadpoles. These have fishlike tails and bulbous heads and will eventually grow legs and turn into fully formed froglets, tiny replicas of the adult. Once they reach this stage, they will need to dodge the dangers of life away from the pond, before returning to mate in a couple of years.

> *Peak migration to breeding sites happens on mild, damp winter and early spring evenings, on a waxing or full moon.*

If you're keen to spot frogs, it's worth paying close attention to the weather and the phases of the moon. Peak migration to breeding sites happens on mild, damp winter and early spring evenings, on a waxing or full moon. Depending on where you live, this could be any time between January (sometimes even December in the far south-west) and April.

Find out where your local pond is and monitor it regularly. Better still, dig a pond in your garden. Small urban ponds are a life-saver for amphibians, offering a combination of year-round cover, food and, of course, water.

Yearly spawning events happen over a few days. If frogs start to gather, take time to sit, watch and listen to them, as they won't be around for long. It will probably be drizzling, and the ground will in all likelihood be wet, so go prepared with waterproofs. Frogs will often disappear if they feel threatened, so approach ponds slowly and carefully. A torch and binoculars come in handy for checking the water from a distance. Frogs' eyes show as eery white orbs in torchlight.

If you're wondering whether the spawn you have found belongs to a frog or a toad, frogspawn looks like staring eyes and is laid in clumps, usually in quite shallow water, while toad spawn looks like a beaded necklace and is most often wrapped around vegetation in slightly deeper water.

Sadly, as with almost half of the UK's wildlife, common frogs aren't as common as their name suggests. What with pesticides that kill the slugs and snails on which they feed, the disappearance of half a million ponds over the last 100 years and a rise in ranavirus, a killer amphibian disease, their long-term survival might be in our hands.

Lesser celandines

Do you ever reach a point in winter when, try as you might, you can't remember what summer felt like? You've been turning on the lights to make your breakfast and drawing the curtains by mid-afternoon for what seems like months. You crave some warmth. Some sunshine. A light at the end of the tunnel. That's when the flowers of the lesser celandine appear.

Once used to treat scurvy, the plant's heart-shaped leaves are full of energy-giving vitamin C as they carpet the ground in lush clumps from late autumn. However, it's when the days lengthen in January that this perennial herb's buttery flowers begin to open, and the ground lights up. Writer D. H. Lawrence once described their flowers as 'pressing themselves at the sun'. When you find one, you'll see that's exactly what they do.

Traditionally, Celandine Day fell on 21 February, when the flowers were supposed to be at their peak. Nowadays, it will depend on where you live, but don't expect this clock-watching plant to open its flowers before 9am or stay open after 5pm.

Considering they're one of the happiest looking flowers, it's a shame they are not appreciated more in the modern world, although this hasn't always been the case. Though synonymous with daffodils, poet William Wordsworth actually favoured lesser celandines. They fascinated him so much he dedicated three poems to them in his lifetime: 'To the Small Celandine', 'To the Same Flower' and 'The Small Celandine'. In floriography – a word used by the Victorians for the language of flowers – the lesser celandine symbolised joys to come and reawakening, which seems an apt description for a flower that shows its face before spring has properly got going.

It's not a big flower. Each bloom has between eight and 12 yellow petals, but is only about 3cm (1¼in) across. It's in the same family as the buttercup, with the scientific name *Ranunculus ficaria*. From the Latin for 'little frog', the genus name no doubt hints at the plant's fondness for damp, marshy ground. In fact, you'll find it growing pretty much everywhere, from parks and gardens to roadsides and woodlands. In places around the world where it has been introduced, it grows so profusely it's even regarded as invasive.

Churchyards are an especially good place to find the lesser celandine. Plants are often found in dense clumps, their open blooms forming a carpet of yellow that's hard to miss on a sunny day. Try to find a quiet spot and sit beside the flowers for a while. Take time to feel their waxy petals. It's a flower that's much loved by pollinators, so if the sun's out, it

*The lesser celandine symbolised joys to come
and reawakening, which seems an apt description for a flower
that shows its face before the spring has properly got going.*

won't be long before a brimstone butterfly or queen bumblebee will come along. Then you can watch how they feed from this source of early nectar; it looks like they are dipping their tongues into a bowl of sunshine.

But don't sit on the damp ground too long. Before more recent developments in medical science, when nature provided remedies for a wide range of ailments, people used a plant's appearance to divine its uses, a concept known as the Doctrine of Signatures. One of the lesser celandine's many common names is 'pilewort'; the resemblance of the plant's roots to haemorrhoids meant that during Tudor times it was commonly used to treat this painful condition.

Happily, two of the lesser celandine's other common names, 'spring messenger' and 'brighteye', do far more justice to this perky little flower. Let's hear it for Wordsworth's 'Little, humble Celandine!'

Great spotted woodpecker

The short, near-silent days of winter can often feel bleak. Nature feels locked away. Unreachable. Our mood, energy levels and mental health can take a battering. So, if you hear the seemingly constant drumming of a great spotted woodpecker echoing through a wood in late winter, it can feel a little surreal.

We know woodpeckers peck wood, the clue is in the name; from excavating nest holes to gaining access to insect larvae, their beaks are obviously vital to their survival. When it comes to protecting their territory and attracting a mate, it's only natural they should use their beak, and at this time of year, the absence of other sounds intensifies the quality and resonance of the hammering.

At speeds of between 10 and 40 pecks per second, great spotted woodpeckers make a point of finding the best sounding trees to drum. The clearer and stronger the sound produced, the more effective it is for warding off rivals and flexing their woodpecker muscles. If we tried something similar, we'd find ourselves in A&E. Yet because of the unique way their beaks are attached to their skulls (via a piece of spongy cartilage), they can drum up to 600 times a day without the slightest risk of damaging their brains.

No wonder then, when engineers needed a way to protect precision instruments, the first thing they turned to for inspiration was the anatomy of the woodpecker. By basing their design on the woodpecker's beak, neck and skull bone, they were able to design a machine that not only absorbed shock, but also helped to reduce vibration, making it possible to keep the sensitive technology inside protected from damage.

It was a more personal story that encouraged Anirudha Surabhi, an industrial designer, to look into a design for a new bicycle helmet that was

launched in 2011. Though he had been wearing a traditional bike helmet, he was still hospitalised with a concussion after a serious accident. Anirudha found that by studying the way the bones in a woodpecker's head stopped the bird's brain from rattling around during impact and understanding how the spongy cartilage acted as a shock-absorber, he was able to develop a bike helmet lining made from air-pocketed recycled paper that softened and absorbed a blow.

At speeds of between 10 and 40 pecks per second, great spotted woodpeckers make a point of finding the best sounding trees to drum.

If you live near woodland, then you'll no doubt have heard a great spotted woodpecker, but now is the time to encounter them properly. In late winter, especially in the morning, their drumming echoes around the trees. Noise carries, so try to work your way closer to the sound. Then it's just a matter of waiting. Although many of us could sit in nature, how many of us do – especially in the winter?

Waiting for a woodpecker to drum is an excellent way to relax, to make some time for yourself. Look around you. Notice what type of leaves are on the ground. Feel the texture of the wood under your fingers and the soft moss and lichens. Look at the way the sun is shining on the bark-less trunk of a fallen log. Search for fungi, from tiny specimens no bigger than your fingernail to ones that smother a dead branch. Or just sit and close your eyes, and as the sound of drumming starts again, as it assuredly will at this time of year, wonder at the complexity of evolution where a creature can smash its beak against a tree repeatedly without getting a headache.

Winter's curiosities

In the early 1600s, a building in Lambeth, London, opened its doors to the public. It was an important milestone. Affectionately called The Ark, it was the first public museum in England, but the collection that lay within its walls hadn't been bequeathed by a rich duke returning from a Grand Tour. Its artefacts were owned by naturalist and gardener, John Tradescant, and were later detailed in a catalogue printed in 1656 with the title *Musaeum Tradescantianum or, A Collection of Rarities*.

For years, a progression of wealthy employers had sent John, and his son (also called John), around the world looking for exotic plants for their gardens, which they had dutifully found, introducing plants such as lilac, gladioli and larch to England. On his travels, he acquired the remains of a dodo, two whale ribs and a brightly coloured parrot, together with thousands of other curios. Upon the death of John the Younger, a

 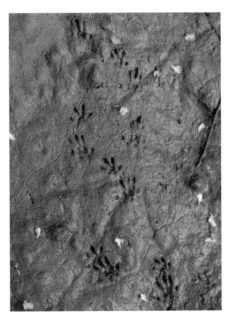

museum was built in Oxford to house the collection, which later became the prestigious Ashmolean Museum.

Nowadays, we understand that we can't all collect natural objects like John Tradescant once did – and it's just as well that we don't. But we can take inspiration from his inquisitiveness towards the natural world.

Winter is the perfect time to find out more about wildlife. When you're less likely to be distracted by spring and summer's vibrant, overgrown lushness and birdsong, or the leaf-muddled russets and browns of autumn. The light can be stark, but this can help the unusual stand out.

Look out for feathers, especially with smudges of iridescent colour or unusual designs. Be more aware of animal prints, large and small, in mud or soft soil. Pay attention to barbed wire on fences, especially where an animal has flattened a path on either side and left a small dip to bob under or through. Are their hairs caught on the wire? Or has a deer shed its yearly antlers while jumping over?

Where an animal has been digging or there's a hole in the ground, look at what has been dug out. You'll sometimes find old bones from past meals or hairs where the animal has been having a scratch (if the strands of hair are black and white and feel triangular when rubbed between your finger and thumb, they're likely to be badger).

Also look for signs of faeces. Most mammal's poo is very distinctive to look at and smell. There's no need to touch it, just push a nearby stick into it, and have a quick sniff (otter poo, sometimes found in prominent positions on rocks next to rivers, is said by some to smell of jasmine tea).

After gales, look for old birds' nests. Have any blown free from their tree-top fixings? Under hazel trees, are there old hazelnut shells? See whether sharp teeth have opened them to gain access to the nut, leaving a telltale gnawed circle (depending on the way it has been opened you can tell what animal opened it).

Take photographs, sketch your finds, make an audio recording, or, if they're small and insignificant enough, take them home, being mindful not to take objects needed by nature, or that are illegal to remove.

Once back in the comfort and warmth of your home, you can begin your detective work. The internet is a vast encyclopaedia of wildlife knowledge. From The Wildlife Trusts' A–Z of species, the Woodland Trust's description of trees, and the Mammal Society's species directory and helpful photos of poo. There's also an infinite number of field guides and books available from bookshops, libraries and charity shops. Equipping yourself with just one good field guide or wildlife identification book will help identify most of your finds.

Then make a special place for your collection. Your very own ark or cabinet of curiosities. From the jay's iridescent blue feather, the windblown, lichen-decorated nest of a chaffinch, to a hazelnut shell gnawed by a wood mouse. Each time you look at them, you'll remember where, when and how you found them. Each one a voyage of discovery into nature's wonders.

Jay feather

Index

acorns 94, 106, 108
adders 25
alder 14
alder buckthorn 18
ants 69–71
Armillaria ostoyae 126
ash 14, 15
Ashmolean Museum
  169–70
aspen 14
autumn gales 119–21

Babcock, Heather 20
badgers 149, 170
*Bambi, a Life in the
  Woods* (Salten) 105
bank voles 84
Bat Conservation
  Trust 53
bats 51–3
beadlet sea anemones
  75–7
Bear, Isabel (Joy) 60
bedeguar gall 100
bee-flies 28–30, 36
beech 14, 15

Big Butterfly Count
  16, 18
bird nests 10–12, 137,
  170
blackbirds 38, 84, 95,
  149
blackcaps 22–4
blackthorn 14, 40, 41,
  94
blossom 40–2
blue tits 10–12, 22
'Bluebell, The' (Brontë)
  43
bluebells 33, 43–5, 158
brimstone butterflies
  16–18, 43, 165
Brontë, Anne 43, 119
buff ermine
  caterpillars 84
bumblebees 19, 28, 50,
  98
Butterfly
  Conservation 16, 18

caching food 106–8
Carroll, Lewis 147

Carson, Rachel 60
Casino Royale 49
catkins 156–8
Celandine Day 163
Centre for Ecology
  and Hydrology 13
chaffinches 144, 171
Chaucer, Geoffrey 109
Chinese water deer
  102, 104, 105
Clare, John 19, 51,
  109
cockchafers 57–9
common frogs 159–62
common lizards 25
common spangle galls
  99, 100
conkers 94, 122–5
crab apple 41, 95
crickets 90–2

da Vinci, Leonardo
  100
daffodils 34
damselflies 78–81
damsons 94

dandelions 19–21, 33, 87
dawn chorus 37–9
'Death of a Naturalist' (Heaney) 159
deer 102–5, 149
dew 85–7
dogwood 14
dormice 84, 95
dragonflies 78–81
drupes 93, 94

elder 15, 82–4
'Emmonsails Heath in Winter' (Clare) 109
ergot 100–1

faeces 170
fallen leaves 113–15
fallow deer 102, 105
feathers 11, 22, 106, 144, 170, 171
field maple 14
fieldfares 94, 95, 109–12
Finding Nemo 77

fly agaric 127
foxes 106, 149
foxgloves 48–50
frogs 159–62
frosts 132–4
fruits 24, 93, 94, 95
fungi 126–9

galls 99–101
Geminids 150, 152
goat willow 14
goldfinches 144, 146
Goodfellow, Robin 100
grass snakes 25, 26
grasshoppers 90–2
great spotted woodpeckers 166–8
great tits 22, 38
greenfinches 144

harlequin ladybirds 73
hawthorn 14, 40–1, 42, 95, 110
hazel 14, 15, 94, 156–8

hazelnuts 94, 122, 156, 158, 170
Heaney, Seamus 159
Hill, Octavia 7
holly 110
holly blue butterfly caterpillars 98
hornbeam 14
horse chestnut 13, 14, 122–5
house martins 109
house sparrows 38, 137
house spiders 116–18
hoverflies 19, 33, 63–5, 98

International Dawn Chorus Day 38
International Dark-Sky Association 150
ivy 96–8
ivy bees 98

jackdaws 38, 135
jays 106–8

ladybirds 72–4
Lawrence, D. H. 163
leaf buds 13–15
lesser celandines
   163–5
London plane 14
Lyrids 150

Macbeth (Shakespeare)
   25
magpies 108
maple 14
marble galls 99
marmalade hoverflies
   63–5
Marsham, Robert 13
meteors 150–2
moles 66–8, 106
money spiders 85, 87
Monty Python and the
   Holy Grail 82
muntjac deer 102, 105
muslin moth
   caterpillars 19

Nature's Calendar
   13–14

noctule bats 51
nuts 93–4, 106

oak 14, 15, 94, 99–100,
   108
oak apple galls 99–100
orb-weaver spider 86

Parliament of Fowls,
   The (Chaucer) 109
Perseid 150
pied wagtails 135, 136
pipistrelle bats 51, 52,
   53
Plath, Sylvia 139
primroses 18, 30, 34

Ratnieks, Francis 96
red admiral butterflies
   98
red deer 102, 105
redwings 109–12
Reeves's muntjac deer
   102
robins 38, 84, 153–5
Robin's pincushion
   100, 101

roe deer 105
rooks 58, 135
roosting 135–7
rose hips 95
rowan 14, 95
ruby tiger moth
   caterpillars 19
'Rural Evening'
   (Clare) 51
rutting deer 102–4

Salten, Felix 105
sand lizards 25
sand martins 109
sea anemones 75–7
seed heads 144–6
shadows 138–40
Shakespeare, William
   25
sika deer 102, 104, 105
sloes 40, 94
slow worms 25–7
'Small Celandine, The'
   (Wordsworth) 163
smells 60–2
smooth snake 25
snow 147–9

solitary bees 19, 28, 30, 31–3
song thrushes 38, 95
spindle 14
spotted wolf spiders 54–6
Stoker, Bram 51
Surabhi, Anirudha 166, 168
swallow-tailed moth caterpillars 98
swallows 109
sweet chestnuts 125
swifts 109
sycamore 14

tawny mining bees 31, 32
tawny owls 141–3
teasels 144, 146
Tennyson, Lord Alfred 78
Thomas, Richard 60
Through the Looking-Glass (Carroll) 147
'To the Same Flower' (Wordsworth) 163

'To the Small Celandine' (Wordsworth) 163
Tradescant, John 169–70
'Two Voices, The' (Tennyson) 78

Victoria, Queen 77

walnut 14, 94
Weizmann, Chaim 124
White, Gilbert 22, 27
white-spotted pug caterpillars 84
wild cherry 14
wild clematis 144
wild pear 41
Withering, William 48
wolves 105
wood anemones 34–6
wood pigeons 38, 149
Woodland Trust 13
Wordsworth, William 163

World Conker Championships 122–3
wrens 37, 38, 135, 137

Picture Credits